Praise for
Your Emotional Fingerprint

"*Your Emotional Fingerprint* is a wonderful tool to discover who you really are at the core, essence level. Life is about self-awareness, self-acceptance, and self-expression, which lead to fulfillment. *Your Emotional Fingerprint* will help you become self-aware and fully express who you are, which will allow you to have more love, wealth, health, and joy in your life. I highly recommend it."

—Jack Canfield, *New York Times* bestselling coauthor of the *Chicken Soup for the Soul* series and author of *The Success Principles*

"The more time I spend with the smartest people and learn their deepest strategies, it all comes back to their Emotional Fingerprint. Woody Woodward has clarified why people do what they do and what makes them successful. This book will show you how to tap into your own Emotional Fingerprint to reach success."

—Garrett B. Gunderson, *New York Times* bestselling author of *Killing Sacred Cows*

"Understanding your Emotional Fingerprint is the source of all extraordinary achievement and will help you achieve your impossible dream."

—Mary Louise Zeller, seventeen-time U.S. national gold medalist in tae kwon do

"As you begin to understand your Emotional Fingerprint and gain insight into yourself, it gives you a greater insight into others. Insight allows you to make a greater impact in life."

—Les Brown, bestselling author of *Live Your Dreams* and *The Power of Purpose*

"Being able to connect on a deep, intimate level by understanding your Emotional Fingerprint will allow you to create wealth in your life, relationships, and business."

—Greg S. Reid, *Wall Street Journal* bestselling coauthor of *Three Feet from Gold*

"In this excellent book, Woody Woodward powerfully clarifies how to positively influence outcomes and behaviors through a richer understanding of a person's Emotional Fingerprint."

—Gary W. Goldstein, producer of *Pretty Woman* and *Under Siege*

"Within five minutes of learning my Emotional Fingerprint I understood why my relationships worked or didn't. It helped me get really clear about what inspired me in my life."

—James Malinchak, coauthor of *Chicken Soup for the Athlete's Soul*

"When you are marketing to someone you must understand his or her Emotional Fingerprint to trigger their buy buttons. Woody Woodward will teach you how to discover your buyer's Emotional Fingerprint and find out what causes him or her to buy more."

—Joel Comm, *New York Times* bestselling author of *Twitter Power*

"By understanding your Emotional Fingerprint you will be able to tap into your inner strength to overcome your challenges, better your relationships, and be more profitable."

—Andrew Hewitt, coauthor of *The Power of Focus for College Students*

"The benefits of discovering and applying the Emotional Fingerprint are almost endless. This book helps readers gain needed insight to overcome personal challenges, improve meaningful relationships, have difficult conversations (without the difficulty), and take the necessary initiative to move forward and achieve their personal and financial goals. It is a book you will read more than once and one you will give to others time and time again."

—Tom Smith, *New York Times* bestselling coauthor of *The Oz Principle, How Did That Happen?*, and *Change the Culture, Change the Game*

Your Emotional Fingerprint

7 Secrets That Will Transform Your Life

WOODY WOODWARD

WILEY
John Wiley & Sons, Inc.

Copyright © 2011 by Woody Woodward. All rights reserved

Design by Forty-five Degree Design LLC

"Emotional Fingerprint" is a registered trademark of Woody Woodward.

Published by John Wiley & Sons, Inc., Hoboken, New Jersey
Published simultaneously in Canada

No part of this publication may be reproduced, stored in a retrieval system, or transmitted in any form or by any means, electronic, mechanical, photocopying, recording, scanning, or otherwise, except as permitted under Section 107 or 108 of the 1976 United States Copyright Act, without either the prior written permission of the Publisher, or authorization through payment of the appropriate per-copy fee to the Copyright Clearance Center, 222 Rosewood Drive, Danvers, MA 01923, (978) 750-8400, fax (978) 646-8600, or on the web at www.copyright.com. Requests to the Publisher for permission should be addressed to the Permissions Department, John Wiley & Sons, Inc., 111 River Street, Hoboken, NJ 07030, (201) 748-6011, fax (201) 748-6008, or online at http://www.wiley.com/go/permissions.

Limit of Liability/Disclaimer of Warranty: While the publisher and the author have used their best efforts in preparing this book, they make no representations or warranties with respect to the accuracy or completeness of the contents of this book and specifically disclaim any implied warranties of merchantability or fitness for a particular purpose. No warranty may be created or extended by sales representatives or written sales materials. The advice and strategies contained herein may not be suitable for your situation. You should consult with a professional where appropriate. Neither the publisher nor the author shall be liable for any loss of profit or any other commercial damages, including but not limited to special, incidental, consequential, or other damages.

For general information about our other products and services, please contact our Customer Care Department within the United States at (800) 762–2974, outside the United States at (317) 572-3993 or fax (317) 572-4002.

Wiley also publishes its books in a variety of electronic formats and by print-on-demand. Some content that appears in standard print versions of this book may not be available in other formats. For more information about Wiley products, visit us at www.wiley.com.

Library of Congress Cataloging-in-Publication Data:
Woodward, Woody, date.
    Your emotional fingerprint : 7 secrets that will transform your life / Woody Woodward. — 1st ed.
        p. cm.
    Includes index.
    ISBN 978-0-470-64011-1 (paper); ISBN 978-1-118-09315-3 (ebk);
    ISBN 978-1-118-09358-0 (ebk); ISBN 978-1-118-09359-7 (ebk)
        1. Emotions. 2. Success. 3. Self-actualization (Psychology) 4. Self-help techniques. I. Title.
    BF531.W663 2011
    152.4—dc23
                                                                    2011036450

OVERTON MEMORIAL LIBRARY
HERITAGE CHRISTIAN UNIVERSITY
P.O. Box HCU
Florence, Alabama 35630

Printed in the United States of America

10 9 8 7 6 5 4 3 2 1

The unconquerable human spirit. I am humbled by the ability of people's willingness to better themselves, their relationships, and their business. This book is dedicated to you. May you find one thing from this book that you can apply to maximize your life.

CONTENTS

ACKNOWLEDGMENTS

Publicly I want to acknowledge the hand of my Heavenly Father in this work. For without his inspiration and guiding influence none of this work would have been accomplished. Personally I want to thank my devoted and inspired wife. My name may be on the cover, but many of these experiences and words came from her. She is my constant and true north. To my kids, who prayed that I may finish early so we could play, may this work be an inspiration to you. To my parents, who have been the greatest example of how to make other people feel important, especially my saintly mother. You are the reason this book came to be. To my other mother and father, I was fortunate enough to be yours after marrying your daughter. Your support over the years has been nothing short of a miracle. To my siblings on both sides of the family, I pull from your example and strength. D.R., without your constant, challenging, and thought-provoking inquiries this message could never have come to pass. You are too internal to have your name in print, but you know where you stand with me and this work. Jeff Roldan, without your gifted talents and commitment to this work I would not be here today. Lindi Stoler, without your constant guiding influence and patience I never would have made this book. Steve Troha, your enthusiasm nurtured this idea from a concept to a worldwide book.

I want to thank everyone at Folio Literary Management, especially Celeste Fine. Rachel Kranz, you were the magic behind the scenes. Your commitment to this message made this book what it is today. To Stefanie Lien, for her contributions in editing and brainstorming. Lori LeBeau-Walsh has been the design maven behind all of my branding. Thank you for understanding me and all of my crazy requests.

It has been a pleasure to work with such an honorable publishing house as John Wiley & Sons. I am grateful for Tom Miller and his long hours of dedication and Lisa Burstiner for her inspired words and insightful editing. In closing, I would like to thank all of my past, present, and future clients. I do this work for you. Thank you for opening your life, heart, and smiles to me.

To learn more about me, visit www.MeetWoody.com. To maximize your emotional fingerprint visit my website www.MyEmotionalFingerprint.com.

How Do You Own Your Life?

Idropped out of high school when I was sixteen. By the time I was twenty-six, I was a millionaire. By age twenty-seven, I was flat broke, living in my parents' basement with my wife and our infant son, three frustrated casualties of the dot-com boom. My wife and I weren't ready to give up, though. During the next five years we created a multimillion-dollar mortgage and real estate firm and did business in seven states. By 2005, we were closing more than thirty million dollars in transactions annually.

Then I saw the writing on the wall: the real estate bubble was going to burst. My wife and I closed our business and sold all of our rental properties. Having gone broke and then making even more money back got me thinking about other people who overcame heart-wrenching trials. I began to research people who had surmounted obstacles in their lives; I was looking for their secrets—not just of their success but also of their extraordinary persistence in the face of hardship. Although my family and I were secure for the time being, I wanted to learn how to handle future ups and downs as well as find some clarity and closure for our past. We had worked hard and were persistent, but I suspected that there was more to lifelong success than that, and I wanted to know what it was.

I ended up reading more than a thousand biographies, from which I wrote a seven-volume series called *Millionaire Dropouts: Inspiring Stories of the World's Most Successful Failures.* The series catalogs the lives of hundreds of men and women who, like me, had dropped out of school at some point and then gone on to achieve measurable success. I was beginning to put together a picture of the kind of person who managed to succeed against all odds—someone committed, flexible, enthusiastic, and patient—but I kept sensing that something was missing.

Then one day my wife came to me in excitement and said, "I've just finished a book that you have to read. It's called *How to Win Friends and Influence People.*"

"Honey, come on," I said. "I can't read one more book."

Nevertheless, my wife, in her infinite wisdom insisted—and thank heavens she did, because that one suggestion changed the rest of our lives. On the first page of the book's second chapter was a quote from the American philosopher and educator John Dewey: "The deepest urge in human nature is the desire to be important."

It's hard to express the multitude of feelings that welled up in me as I stared at those words: shock, elation, bewilderment, curiosity. I had a lot of conflicting thoughts, too: "That's ridiculous! *I* don't want to be important!" "What does he mean by 'important,' exactly?" "It sounds like he's saying everyone's an egotist. What about Gandhi? Or Harriet Tubman? Did *they* want to be important?" Underneath my resistance was another, smaller voice that continued to grow: "This is it! This is the missing link I've been searching for."

Even though I didn't quite understand what Dewey meant, somehow I knew that he was on to something. I realized that the desire to be important was indeed behind all of the success stories I had studied and written about, but I also understood that when Dewey talked about people wanting to be important, he wasn't saying that they needed to be praised, honored, or even recognized for their good qualities. He wasn't talking about being the best, winning a gold medal, or becoming famous. He was saying that people need to believe that they *matter*, that they are *significant*. People need to believe that they have found their place in the world, that they are exactly where they belong and are doing exactly what they're supposed to be doing.

Each of us acquires a sense of importance in a different way. Some of us get it from relationships with a romantic partner, friends, and/or family. Some of us get it from looking our best, from working out, or from visiting a place we've never been before and learning something new. Some of us achieve a sense of importance from extraordinary public accomplishments. Some of us get it from simply being good parents.

"The deepest urge in human nature is the desire to be important." At the time, I didn't know what Dewey meant, but I was suddenly on fire with the need to find out. I got up from my chair, dashed to my car, and called my wife on my cell phone. "Honey, I'm going to be late tonight," I told her. "There's something I have to do."

I drove to the local university and started interviewing anyone I could find: students, professors, librarians, anybody who was willing to talk to me. "What makes you feel important?" I asked each person, and I wrote down their answers.

That hectic day of interviewing led to another, then another, then still another. I eventually traveled to find people in more unusual situations and in vastly different walks of life. I sought out all types of people, from prisoners to priests, doctors to dancers, businesspeople to bricklayers. I spoke with celebrities and homeless people, PhDs and high school dropouts, entrepreneurs and union members. No matter whom I talked to or where I went, I kept finding more and more evidence for the same point: Dewey was right. The deepest urge in human nature *is* the desire to feel important.

I discovered something else, too. When you reduce the feeling to its basics, there are always seven characteristics, or *aspects of importance*, that make someone feel important. My seven may be different from your seven, but we each have seven aspects of importance. These seven aspects make up your *emotional fingerprint*.

Your emotional fingerprint is the driving force behind why you do what you do. It is what influences your emotional highs and lows and thus creates your good days and your bad days. Have you ever wondered what makes you feel on top of the world one day and completely depressed the next? Why do some people drive you completely crazy whereas others are so easy to be around? Why are you attracted to one person and turned off by someone else? Why do you enjoy doing some things and hate doing others?

The answers to each of these questions is a reflection of your unique emotional fingerprint. Your emotional fingerprint affects your moods, your decisions, the outcome of your relationships, and, ultimately, your failures and your successes. In fact, understanding your emotional fingerprint is the key to owning your life.

When I discovered the concept of the emotional fingerprint, a whole new world opened up to me. I realized that *becoming aware of* your emotional fingerprint enables you to master your emotional highs and lows. I learned that your emotional compass guides you in choosing to validate aspects of your emotional fingerprint. I understood that becoming aware of your emotional fingerprint is the key to creating a happy, successful life.

When you are aware of your emotional fingerprint, you can ask yourself to acknowledge—with rigorous, ruthless honesty—exactly what choices you're making and why you're making them. Not having this type of self-awareness always gets us into trouble. For example, a woman might believe that she's spontaneous and independent, someone who values her freedom above anything else. But if she understood her emotional fingerprint, she might realize that it is only the *idea* of freedom and independence that she likes, that what really makes her feel important is security and commitment. This awareness might lead her to choose a romantic partner who also values security and commitment, rather than running after the free-spirited types who inevitably disappoint her. As I explain in chapters 1, 2, and 3, becoming aware of your emotional fingerprint can help you to make better decisions. In fact, that awareness is the first step to owning our lives.

Being aware of your emotional fingerprint is not enough, however. Both the people I interviewed and the ones whose biographies I read had taken another important step: *internalizing* their emotional fingerprints.

Internalizing your emotional fingerprint means understanding that no matter what your situation, you always have a choice. Suppose your boss tells you that you have to do something that is borderline unethical or risk losing your job. That's a lousy spot to be in, but it does include a choice. You might not like either alternative, but you still have the power to choose between them. Or suppose that the spouse you love informs you that he or she wants a divorce. You may not have the choice to hold on to your beloved, but you can choose how you'll handle the breakup. The psychotherapist and concentration camp survivor Viktor Frankl said, "Everything can be taken from a man or a woman but one thing: the last of human freedoms—to choose one's attitude in any given set of circumstances, to choose one's own way."

There's more to internalizing your emotional fingerprint. You must also understand that no matter how the external world treats you, you can always choose to validate *yourself.* The most effective way to validate yourself is to understand your emotional finger-print and actively affirm your seven aspects of importance.

If you are a person who feels important when in a loving relationship, for example, rather than looking to your spouse or romantic partner whom you love for validation, look to yourself. Become someone who does a good job of giving and receiving love, and feel important because of your own relationship skills rather than because of your partner's response. If you are a person who feels important when being praised, find ways to praise yourself. Seek ways to affirm your seven aspects of importance yourself so that you are never dependent on the outside world for validation.

The choice to rely on internal rather than external validation is what gives successful people their extraordinary emotional reserves. The people I studied each had a depth of strength and fortitude that kept them on their paths despite enormous obstacles. Entrepreneurs weathered bankruptcies and recessions, political leaders survived lost elections and changing times, and spiritual figures persevered despite scorn and persecution. What made them so resilient was the capacity to internalize their emotional fingerprints through the processes I explain in chapters 4, 5, and 6.

Once you have internalized your emotional fingerprint, there's only one more step: to maximize it. Learn to clear your path of fears and anxieties by letting go of the future and living in the present. Clarify your standards so that you are making decisions you can be proud of, regardless of the results. Sharpen your resolve so that you see clearly what you can affect in a situation, then take positive targeted action to get what you want.

Once you follow these three steps—becoming aware of, internalizing, and maximizing your emotional fingerprint—you will own your life, because you will always know what makes you feel important, how to validate yourself, and which actions will serve your best self.

Living this way inevitably produces extraordinary results. After I developed the concept of the emotional fingerprint, I began a successful coaching business, and I've helped thousands of clients find success—in their personal lives, in their relationships, and in their careers. I've helped my clients find new love, revitalize old relationships, earn promotions, negotiate deals, and start new businesses. Some of my clients develop their hobbies and avocations into successful new careers. Others find new ways to become better parents. Still others say that they've regained their enthusiasm for a life that had grown dull and flat.

To better understand how your emotional fingerprint affects your life, consider Sarah, a woman who is in dire straits. She has lost her job or is afraid that she's likely to lose it soon. Her current relationship is in jeopardy, and she's trying to imagine how she'll face life as a single woman. Her brother has just been laid off from his job, has defaulted on his mortgage, and has moved in with their parents, who have just lost a big chunk of their retirement income and are facing severe medical problems. Sarah's oldest son has learning disabilities, and she can't afford a tutor. Her youngest daughter is starting to run with a bad crowd and is maybe having unsafe sex or doing dangerous drugs. Sarah is dogged by a persistent sense of failure in all areas: relationships, work, and family life. "How did everything turn out so badly?" she wonders. "And what do I do now?"

Understanding her emotional fingerprint and internalizing it will give Sarah the emotional reserves to triumph over tragedy. No matter how painful her circumstances, she can make the choices that will enable her to change some parts of her situation, accept others, and emerge a stronger, more successful person. By maximizing her emotional fingerprint, Sarah will find a way to make it through the hard times and maybe even create something good from them: stronger and deeper relationships, a more satisfying job, or a new faith in herself.

Also consider Paul, a man whose life seems stale. He's been married for about ten years, and although he and his wife don't fight much, he's not attracted to her the way he once was, and they don't seem to have much to talk about. He has a five-year-old son, whom he loves, but he rarely sees him because of all the long hours Paul spends at work, which he doesn't enjoy but which he feels he must put in to keep his job. He used to love to play tennis, but now he can't find the time to get to the courts. He was once a very good amateur photographer, but lately he hasn't felt like taking pictures, either.

Becoming aware of his emotional fingerprint, internalizing it, and maximizing it will enable Paul to turn an ordinary life into an extraordinary life. He can renew his relationship with his wife, reconnect to his son, and make choices about balancing work and family life that fit his own standards for the man he wants to be. He can also rediscover his enthusiasm for the activities that used to nourish him, or discover new activities and new passions. Instead of feeling like a boring burden, Paul's "ordinary" life will come to feel like an extraordinary gift.

Does this sound like a lot to expect? It is, and I encourage you to expect it. I've seen this approach work with the clients I coach and with the thousands of people who attend my seminars and training sessions. I've seen it work for the great men and women

I wrote about, and I've seen it work for me and my family. Understanding, internalizing, and maximizing your emotional fingerprint will launch you on a journey that may be the most thrilling trip you ever take. So let's get started. All you have to do is be open to the possibility that you can own your life.

PART I

Become Aware of Your Emotional Fingerprint

1

Discover Your Emotional Fingerprint

Be yourself; everyone else is already taken.
—Oscar Wilde

Don't touch that!" the security guard yelled. I slowly removed my finger from *Sunflowers*, a painting by Vincent van Gogh. Earlier that day I had been looking at a pair of Oakley sunglasses, and it seemed as though I had to give the sales clerk a photo ID, my Social Security number, and the deed to my house just to get him to take the glasses out of the store's display case. Now, here at the New York Metropolitan Museum of Modern Art, I was staring at a seemingly unprotected priceless and world-famous piece of art. I knew I wasn't supposed to touch it, but the impulse to make contact with even a sliver of something so precious was too much for me to withstand.

If my wife had been with me, I guarantee you that she would not have touched that painting in a million years, even if she knew the security guard was nowhere to be found. She would have marveled at the art just as much as I did, she would have loved the experience of viewing it, and she would have emerged from the museum with a deeper, richer appreciation of the extraordinary painting and the artist who created it. She would never have broken the museum's rules, however, whereas I, even with the security guard standing right there, couldn't keep myself from breaking them.

Why are we different this way? What makes one person accepting and respectful of rules and restrictions while another person has to push the limits and oppose authority? What makes one person able to deeply appreciate a piece of art, whereas another person shrugs and moves on? What makes my logic and my view of right and wrong so compelling to me even though your approach to the world—perhaps very different from mine—seems equally correct and compelling to you?

The answer, I believe, can be found in our emotional fingerprints.

What Is an Emotional Fingerprint?

Your emotional fingerprint is a blueprint of your deepest desires and strongest feelings. It explains why you respond the way you do, both positively and negatively, to the people and events in your life. Becoming aware of your emotional fingerprint enables you to make conscious, effective decisions so that you can get what you want, overcome challenges, and find the happiness you seek. Becoming aware of other people's emotional fingerprints allows you to deal with them more effectively, in your personal life, your relationships, and your work life.

Your emotional fingerprint is based on your feelings of importance. By *importance*, I don't mean ego, selfishness, acclaim, or recognition; I mean your own sense of "Yes! I'm doing the right thing at the right time. I'm exactly where I'm supposed to be. I feel enthusiastic and at peace."

To understand what I mean by important, think of an instance in which you felt on top of the world. I'm not talking about an ordinary good day or even an unusually good day; I'm talking about a peak experience, when you felt absolutely incredible.

You might be imagining a moment of great success or professional recognition, such as winning an award or receiving great applause when speaking. It might be a moment of huge personal triumph: becoming engaged, signing the mortgage on your dream house, or watching your child graduate from college.

You might instead be imagining a far more humble, private moment. Perhaps you're thinking of a country walk you took one night, when you looked up at the stars and felt suddenly awed by their beauty. Maybe you're thinking of the day you gave a stranger a helping hand and felt a rush of joy from being of service. You might be remembering a winter vacation when you skied down a snowy mountain, exulting in every thrilling second, or a morning when you finished your daily jog in a blissful glow of good health. Perhaps you're recalling being flooded with love at the sight of your toddler coloring or the sound of your infant cooing.

These peak experiences were so precious and satisfying because you felt important. As you can see from the examples, importance, in this sense, is not necessarily about being successful or being better than someone else. It might involve achievement, recognition, praise, or triumph, but it doesn't have to. It might involve the presence of another person or of several people, but that isn't necessary, either.

When you feel important, you feel connected to who you really are. Feeling important brings with it a sense of completion and wholeness, as though you have so much that you couldn't possibly want any more. "This is absolutely perfect," you think. Just looking at the stars, skiing down the mountain, or watching your child feels satisfying enough. Feeling important means that you feel on top of the world. It means feeling connected, loved, appreciated, or significant in your life. It means feeling elated, enthusiastic, fulfilled, and full of joy from being in your purpose. It is a deep-down knowledge that all is well and that you are in the right place at the right time. We all have peak emotional highs when we feel absolutely incredible. That is a feeling of importance.

There are thirty-five universal feelings of importance, but each of us has seven primary areas in which we feel important. These seven areas, or characteristics of importance, make up a person's emotional fingerprint.

Everyone's emotional fingerprint is unique, partly because we don't all share the same areas of importance. Your peak experiences made *you* feel important. Another person might have had the same experiences and been only mildly happy or even had a negative response. My emotional fingerprint includes being free and independent, so I was moved to touch the painting in the museum. For me, it wasn't enough to follow the rules and stand there obediently—I had to enjoy the painting in my own way. My wife, in contrast, feels important when she is living in the moment—that's part of her emotional fingerprint—so she doesn't have the same need to oppose authority and make her own rules. For her, just looking at the picture would have been enough, whereas trying to bend the rules would have spoiled the moment for her. Each of us has his or her own aspects of importance and his or her own emotional fingerprint.

When I am coaching a new client, sometimes we run into a little trouble with the notion of importance. Because of the many associations that people have with that word, they may think that it involves being egotistical, proud, boastful, or self-centered; it doesn't. They may think that it's about being better than somebody else; it isn't. A feeling of importance has nothing to do with thinking that you are the best, that you're entitled to something, or that you have anything that others do not. A feeling of importance is simply a deep sense of connection to who you really are, a feeling of confidence that everything is just as it should be.

Another type of confusion arises when clients think that I'm talking about what is important *to* them rather than when they *feel* important. To clear up the confusion, I might say, "Your job may be important *to* you, but does it make you *feel* important?" Often the answer is no. Or perhaps "Your family may be important *to* you, but does it make you *feel* important?" Again the answer is sometimes no. Whatever makes you *feel* important is an element of your emotional fingerprint.

Identifying Your Emotional Fingerprint

Seven primary aspects of importance make up your emotional fingerprint. Knowing your emotional fingerprint gives you a way to quickly visualize the core pillars of your personality and, ultimately, to become aware of what you really want from your life. When you know your emotional fingerprint, you've taken the first step to owning your life.

To identify your emotional fingerprint, take the following simple quiz. It's based on five years of research that I conducted with the help of several colleagues, interviewing more than twenty-five hundred people from all walks of life to see what made them feel important. We interviewed a diverse group of people of both sexes from different backgrounds, races, and educational levels. We also catalogued the responses of thousands more people from our websites, e-mail, and social networking sites. All of this research enabled us to determine the primary situations in which people feel important.

It is interesting to note that among all of the people we interviewed, we never found anyone who said that he or she felt important from having lots of money, drinking, taking drugs, watching pornography, gambling, or engaging in promiscuous sex. As we'll see in part 2, people do sometimes turn to these escapes to manufacture a false sense of importance or to avoid the feeling of being unimportant. Nevertheless, no one—not even the people who *are* involved in these activities—considers them core areas of importance.

For the questionnaires and exercises in this book, either fill them in here or use a separate notebook to record your answers.

To fill in the following questionnaire online or to share it with your friends go to www.MyEmotionalFingerprint.com.

QUESTIONNAIRE

Determining Your Emotional Fingerprint

1. Read through the thirty-five feelings of importance described in the seven groups below. Don't judge them or compare them or even apply them to yourself. Just read through them.

2. After you've read through them once, go through them again group by group. Select only *one* item in each group that enables you to complete the sentence "I feel important when I am _____

_____."

You may want to choose two or more items from the same group, but please choose only one. If you're having trouble choosing, ask yourself which would prevail in case of a conflict. For example, in group 1, you will find "[I feel important when I am] in control" and "[I feel important when I am] organized." You may enjoy both being in control and being organized, so to make the choice, picture a conflict such as the following: You've just moved into a new office, and everything is completely disorganized. You have the opportunity to lead a new work team, but it will mean leaving your office in disarray for quite a while. When you picture the two alternatives—leading a team that you're in control of but having a messy office, or organizing your office before you take on any new responsibilities—which makes you happier? Which situation would you choose? That's the situation that makes you feel more important, so mark it down in that group.

Another way to choose when a decision is close is to ask yourself which of the two experiences you could not live without. So, using the same example, even though you might like both being in control and being organized, if you had to choose, would you rather live without control or without being organized?

Finally, if possible, base your choice on your first impression—just pick whichever answer seems to leap out at you. You may be tempted to think about what your choices mean or what they say about you, but I urge you to resist that temptation. You'll have time to think about your answers after I've had the chance to explain a bit more about how they work. As you gain more clarity, you'll certainly be free to come back and change an answer. For now, however, don't think or analyze; simply respond.

Group 1

I feel important when I am

In control

> Examples: Having control in your life, in your job, in a situation, or in a conversation

Confident in my appearance

> Examples: Looking your best, defining your style, or having a unique look

Organized

> Examples: Cleaning, organizing, or putting things in order

Connected to God, spirit, or the universe

> Examples: Feeling inspired, connected, or faithful

Trusted

> Examples: Living so that you are worthy of trust, trusting yourself, having people trust you, or being relied on

My choice from group 1: _____

Group 2

I feel important when I am

Providing

> Examples: Providing financial, emotional, or spiritual support for your family; securing a financial future; or giving to charities

Overcoming challenges

> Examples: Overcoming obstacles and challenges in projects, in relationships, or in daily life

In the moment

> Examples: Being emotionally present, feeling a deep acceptance of your life, or being centered and connected

In a loving relationship

> Examples: Feeling love for your spouse, partner, loved ones, friends, or yourself

Given respect

> Examples: Feeling respected at home, in your work, or from your friends, or feeling a sense of self-respect

My choice from group 2: _____

Group 3

I feel important when I am

Working

> Examples: Working in a career, at home, or on a serious hobby or avocation

Free and independent

> Examples: Having free time, feeling free of obligations, having the chance to make decisions at work, or feeling independent within a loving relationship or friendship

Relying on my knowledge

> Examples: Using your intelligence to accomplish a task, sharing your knowledge with others, or understanding how things work

Being a friend

> Examples: Spending time calling, texting, or e-mailing friends; maintaining friendships over time; or socializing with friends

Receiving praise

> Examples: Being acknowledged for a job well done by others or yourself, or being appreciated for personal qualities by others or yourself

My choice from group 3: _____

Group 4

I feel important when I am

Secure

> Examples: Being able to count on yourself, your relationship, your finances, or your work

Being creative

> Examples: Expressing your creativity through painting, singing, writing, making a scrapbook, or decorating your home

Healthy

> Examples: Eating right, exercising, losing weight, or living in a healthy way

Connected to family

> Examples: Being with children, grandchildren, parents, siblings, or relatives

Receiving recognition

> Examples: Being recognized for the important role you play at work, at home, or with friends, or recognizing yourself for a job well done or a relationship that you have maintained

My choice from group 4: _____

Group 5

I feel important when I am

Solving problems

> Examples: Fixing things, figuring out solutions at work or to other people's personal problems, organizing projects, or coming up with mechanical solutions

Achieving my life's purpose

> Examples: Fulfilling the reason you believe you are here on earth, carrying out your life's mission, or serving something greater than yourself

Connected to nature

> Examples: Camping, hiking, gardening, walking by the ocean, spending time with animals, protecting the environment, or being "green"

In a position of influence

> Examples: Being a leader, a boss, a politician, or an entrepreneur, or being persuasive

Validated

> Examples: Your view, opinion, or advice is being sought or validated by others, or you affirm your own clarity or insight

My choice from group 5: _____

Group 6

I feel important when I am

Reaching my goals

> Examples: Accomplishing a task, closing a deal, or achieving a desired result

Performing

> Examples: Teaching, singing, dancing, entertaining, or speaking in public

Learning

> Examples: Reading, studying, or learning something new

Being a good parent

> Examples: Taking care of the needs of your child, playing a parental role with young people or students, or being a mentor

Needed

> Examples: People want to spend time with you, others rely on you, or you rely on yourself

My choice from group 6: _____

Group 7
I feel important when I am

Winning

> Examples: Coming out ahead in games, work situations, or personal situations, or believing that you are winning at life

Experiencing life

> Examples: Traveling, exploring, trying new things, being adventurous

Honoring my standards

> Examples: Being true to your moral code, having integrity and principles, being honest, or holding yourself and/or others to certain ideas about how people should behave

Serving

> Examples: Giving and helping or contributing to society, family, or work

Accepted

> Examples: Accepting yourself or being accepted by friends, your family, or your coworkers

My choice from group 7: _____

3. Now record your answers from each group in the following table:

> My emotional fingerprint
>
> I feel important when I am
>
> Group 1_____
>
> Group 2_____
>
> Group 3_____
>
> Group 4_____
>
> Group 5_____
>
> Group 6_____
>
> Group 7_____

The seven feelings you have selected are your seven aspects of importance. These seven aspects make up your unique emotional fingerprint.

Seven Simple Aspects of Importance, One Complex Emotional Fingerprint

At this point you may be wondering how seven simple answers are enough to define your entire personality. After all, you are a complex and multidimensional person. How can you be summed up by only seven responses?

That's what's so exciting about understanding your emotional fingerprint. It gives you a shortcut—a blueprint, so to speak—that allows you to grasp your core concerns very quickly and to rapidly analyze whether a situation validates or offends your aspects of importance.

If you're surprised that only seven feelings of importance can combine to produce something so complex, I invite you to look at some other examples of a few simple systems with remarkable powers of expression. There are only 26 letters in the English alphabet, for example, yet those letters are able to form the estimated 754,000 words that make up our language. Likewise, although we have only ten digits, zero through nine, those few numerals can create infinite numbers. Even our DNA, the genetic code for life itself, is made up of only six nucleic acid bases, yet each of us has a different inheritance. Finally, we each have two eyes, two ears, a nose, and a mouth, but every face is unique.

Thus, even though we all have seven aspects in our emotional fingerprints, our individual interpretation of each aspect is unique. Even if you share the same seven aspects with someone else, you will express them through different feelings, thoughts, and actions. For me, touching the van Gogh painting was an expression of feeling free and independent. Another person might express the same aspect of her emotional fingerprint by leaving the world-famous van Gogh painting to seek out the work of an obscure painter whom no one else recognized. A third person with the same aspect of importance might decide that even being in the museum is too restrictive and instead create his own viewing experience at a number of smaller art galleries. All of us would be expressing the same free and independent aspect of our emotional fingerprints, but each of us would be expressing it in his or her own way.

Your Emotional Fingerprint and Love

Let's see how your emotional fingerprint influences your experience of romantic love and partnership. For simplicity's sake, let's look at only the five aspects of importance in group 1. Notice how each aspect leads to a different interpretation of what love means and when we feel loved.

If you chose being in control, you may need to feel in control to feel loved. This can consist of telling your romantic partner what you want and expecting to get it, feeling in control of your romantic life, or remaining in control of yourself even when the relationship is at its most challenging. If you feel this sense of control, then your aspect of control is being validated, and you feel loved.

If you chose feeling confident in your appearance, you may need to feel confident in your appearance to feel loved. Perhaps you feel loved when your romantic partner acknowledges how beautiful or handsome you are or finds other ways to appreciate your appearance. Perhaps your partner supports your desire to work out, eat in a healthy way, shop for nice clothes, get manicures, or otherwise work on your appearance.

If you chose being organized, then the person who loves you should understand that you need to feel organized to feel important. He or she should make space for this need by accommodating your wishes to organize the space you share, giving you gifts that help you to organize your work space or your time, and respecting the organization you have set up.

If you chose being connected to God, spirit, or the universe, you might share a religious faith with your loved one, or perhaps you share activities that help you to feel a spiritual connection, such as listening to music, hiking in the woods, doing yoga, or meditating. Your partner might help you to feel loved by discussing your own sense of connection with you, encouraging you to take time for whatever feeds your spirituality, or sharing his or her own thoughts on spirituality and religion.

If you chose being trusted, your partner should affirm his or her trust in you, remind you of others who trust you, encourage you to see yourself as trustworthy, or support you in your efforts to build trust with someone else.

If you are not feeling loved, take a look at the seven aspects of your emotional fingerprint and ask yourself how they are being ignored or devalued in your love relationship, or at least how they might be more fully validated there. This will give you a targeted, focused way to identify what is really bothering you and point you toward what you can do to make things better.

Although you might enjoy one of the other aspects of importance in each group, none will make you feel as important as the specific aspect of your emotional fingerprint. If you feel important when you feel trusted, and your husband compliments you on your appearance, that might make you feel good, but it won't make you feel nearly as loved as when he reminds you how deeply he trusts you, either by expressing his trust in words or by taking actions that show how much he trusts you.

Similarly, if your girlfriend lets you take charge of the activities for your next date, you might enjoy the feeling of being in control. However, if being in control isn't part of your emotional fingerprint and being organized is, she would do better to put your DVDs back in alphabetical order, the way you like them, or buy you a new file box for your home office so you can organize it, as you've been meaning to do.

Now let's make it personal. Let's see how your emotional fingerprint determines *your* experience of love.

How Do I Feel Love?

1. Write down the seven aspects of your emotional fingerprint.
2. Look at each aspect of importance. Ask yourself what it tells you about how you experience love. Use my example:

My Emotional Fingerprint

1. Feeling connected to God, spirit, or the universe
2. Providing
3. Being free and independent
4. Being creative
5. Achieving my life's purpose
6. Being a good parent
7. Experiencing life

I feel love in my relationships when I am

1. Feeling connected to God, spirit, or the universe. My wife and I attend church with our kids, and we have scripture study before school.
2. Providing. My kids and my wife talk about our business with me, and we are all working together for the greater good.
3. Free and independent. My wife gives me free time to do whatever I want. She honors me for being unique and independent.
4. Being creative. The kids and I do creative things together on Saturday morning, such as oil paintings, chalk drawings on the driveway, or craft projects.
5. Achieving my life's purpose. My family supports everything I am trying to achieve in my career and my personal life.
6. Being a good parent. We have pizza delivered and watch a movie on Friday night, and we read stories at bedtime.
7. Experiencing life. We travel, go to the beach or to theme parks, and just experience everything around us.

My Emotional Fingerprint

1. _____

2. _____

3. _____

4. _____

5. _____

6. _____

7. _____

I feel love in my relationships when I am

1. _____
_____

2. _____
_____

3. _____
_____

4. _____
_____

5. _____
_____

6. _____
_____

7. _____
_____

Are you starting to get a picture of how your emotional fingerprint reveals your unique experience and points you toward the things you really want? Remember, even if the seven aspects of your emotional fingerprint are the same as those of another person, each of you will have his or her own ways of interpreting those aspects.

Here is an example of someone who has the same emotional fingerprint that I do, yet his life is very different from mine. I'm an entrepreneur and a life coach who has three children with my wife of fifteen years. Jeremy is a freelance writer who's been married twice, with two kids from one of those marriages. He's currently dating a woman with whom things are just starting to get serious. Here's how he responded to the exercise you just completed:

My Emotional Fingerprint

1. Feeling connected to God, spirit, or the universe
2. Providing
3. Being free and independent
4. Being creative
5. Achieving my life's purpose
6. Being a good parent
7. Experiencing life

I feel love in my relationships when I am

1. Connected to God, spirit, or the universe. My girlfriend and I attend yoga classes together. We discuss our ideas about spirit, soul, and life after death.
2. Providing. I provide my girlfriend with the emotional support she needs after a long, hard day, and I often give her a neck rub or a foot rub.
3. Free and independent. When my girlfriend and I travel together, we often take a day to each go off separately and explore. Then we have dinner at night and talk about our adventures.
4. Being creative. I talk about the articles I'm working on with my girlfriend. I also am creative in planning special times for us.
5. Achieving my life's purpose. When I slip from the path to my life's purpose, my girlfriend calls me on it and asks me how I plan to get back on track.
6. Being a good parent. My girlfriend and I talk about my kids. Sometimes she helps me to see some ways to have a better relationship with them.
7. Experiencing life. Every Sunday we try to do something we've never done before, like going to a new part of the

city, finding a new activity, or even just trying out a new restaurant.

As you can see, everyone's interpretation of his or her emotional fingerprint is unique. Knowing the seven aspects that make you feel important—and your own unique interpretation of them—is the key to being aware of your emotional fingerprint.

Your Emotional Fingerprint and Work

We've seen how your emotional fingerprint is expressed in your relationships. What about your work life and your career? Whether you are the CEO of a Fortune 500 company or running your household as a stay-at-home parent, your emotional fingerprint affects how you experience—or fail to experience—fulfillment in your chosen work. Looking at only the five aspects of importance in group 2, you can see many ways in which your emotional fingerprint might affect your work life.

Providing
You might interpret providing as

- Providing financially for yourself and your family
- Securing a financial future
- Giving to charity
- Providing yourself, your family, your community, or the world with some nonfinancial benefit: emotional assistance, intellectual insight, spiritual connection, physical improvement, or support for health

Overcoming challenges
You might interpret challenges as

- Making more money for yourself, your department, or your company
- Creating or promoting a product or a service that is widely respected and appreciated
- Helping everyone in your department or your company to get along

- Encouraging everyone in your department or your company to be more productive
- Being a troubleshooter
- Dealing with schedules, deadlines, or a long to-do list
- Overcoming a personal challenge, such as shyness in making cold calls
- Being reluctant to take on authority or holding your temper with the office grouch
- Helping your kids get what they need
- Coping with a spouse or a romantic partner who is out of work or struggling with another serious problem

Living in the moment
Your work-related version of living in the moment might involve

- Being present and emotionally available to clients, colleagues, or members of your household
- Accepting what is: a difficult boss, a frustrating policy change, or an economic problem
- Confronting setbacks at home
- Being centered and connected in everything you do

Being in a loving relationship
While engaged in your work or career, you might turn to thoughts of your loving relationship to help you

- Regain your emotional equilibrium when things go badly
- Muster the courage to take new risks
- Give of yourself to do your best work

Being given respect
At work, you might interpret respect as being

- Paid what you believe you deserve
- Given the responsibilities you believe you deserve

- Asked for your opinion
- Given respect for being a stay-at-home parent
- Spoken to respectfully rather than ordered around

To make this personal, complete the following exercise. How does your emotional fingerprint affect your feelings about work and career?

EXERCISE

How Do I Feel Fulfilled in My Work?

1. Look again at the seven aspects of importance of your emotional fingerprint that you wrote down for the first exercise.

2. Ask yourself what each aspect tells you about what you're looking for in your work life. Use the example of Maria Vasquez, a marketing consultant, as a guide:

I feel fulfilled at work when I am

1. Trusted. I love it when my clients and my colleagues trust me. I'd go to any lengths to do a good job for a client who has given me his or her trust.

2. In the moment. When I get all wrapped up in a meeting to figure out a client's needs, I forget about everything else.

3. Free and independent. My job lets me make a lot of decisions myself. I come up with the marketing plan, and I have a lot of control over when and where I meet with clients and how I schedule my own work.

4. Secure. I feel secure when I know I've gotten all the information I need and there won't be any surprises.

5. Solving problems. I like solving problems for my clients.

6. Reaching my goals. I work hard to reach my goals, but that's something I enjoy.

7. Serving. I love feeling of service to my clients and to the woman in charge of our department, who has been very good to me.

I feel fulfilled at work when I am

1. _____
   _____

2. _____
   _____

3. _____
   _____

4. _____
   _____

5. _____
   _____

6. _____
   _____

7. _____
   _____

Do you see how much your emotional fingerprint reveals about you in your work? Knowing your emotional fingerprint allows you to be conscious of what you need so that you can take effective steps to get more of what you want.

When Something Isn't Going Right

Your emotional fingerprint doesn't identify only the sources of fulfillment in your life. It also helps you to understand why something is *not* working, so that you can target your actions to make it right. To learn more about how your emotional fingerprint can help you to analyze problems in your life, complete the next exercise.

EXERCISE

What's Not Working Well Right Now?

1. Choose an area where you are feeling frustrated, whether in your relationships, at work, or in your personal life. Write down what

is bothering you as specifically as you can, such as "Mike never remembers to take out the garbage" or "My boss isn't paying me enough."

2. Look at the list of your emotional fingerprint aspects of importance that you wrote previously. Ask yourself how each aspect is or is not being met in the situation you're considering. Write down your responses. Use the example of Dava Miller, age thirty-five, who has been in a steady relationship for two years, as a guide:

My Emotional Fingerprint

1. Being trusted
2. Being given respect
3. Relying on my knowledge
4. Feeling secure
5. Connected to nature
6. Being a good parent
7. Honoring my standards

My frustration: My boyfriend never plans dates with me ahead of time; he just comes over and hangs out. I don't mind doing that some of the time, but sometimes I want him to plan a nice evening for us.

How my emotional fingerprint is or is not being met

1. Being trusted: I don't feel trusted; I feel taken for granted. Maybe he doesn't trust me enough to plan something special because he's afraid I won't like it or will make fun of him.
2. Being given respect: I think it shows a lack of respect for me to just treat me like a buddy he can hang out with. If he had more respect for me, he would plan something special once in a while.
3. Relying on my knowledge: Doesn't apply.
4. Feeling secure: I feel insecure when he puts so little effort into our relationship. Doesn't he love me? Doesn't he care about making me happy?
5. Feeling connected to nature: Doesn't apply.
6. Being a good parent: If we get more serious and start a family, is he going to be this way with our kids' birthdays and special days? That's not the kind of father I want my kids to have.

7. Honoring my standards: If I let him treat me this way, I am not meeting my own standards for how I deserve to be treated.

Now it's your turn.

My frustration: _____

How my emotional fingerprint is or is not being met

1. _____

How this aspect is or is not being met

_____

_____

2. _____

How this aspect is or is not being met

_____

_____

3. _____

How this aspect is or is not being met

_____

_____

4. _____

How this aspect is or is not being met

_____

_____

5. _____

How this aspect is or is not being met

_____

_____

6. _____

How this aspect is or is not being met

_____

_____

7. _____

How this aspect is or is not being met

_____

_____

We'll look more at how to respond to situations like these in subsequent chapters. Meanwhile, has this exercise given you any new ideas for how to improve your situation, either by communicating with someone else or by taking new action yourself? If you like, explore these ideas further by writing about them for a few minutes.

Which Type Are You?

At this point you might be wondering if there is a shortcut—a way to identify a particular "type" based on the seven aspects you have identified. Does your emotional fingerprint have a name? Can it fit into a category?

The answer is both yes and no. When I first discovered the concept of the emotional fingerprint, I was very resistant to creating labels. I wanted my clients to look at every aspect of the emotional fingerprints separately, because, as you will see throughout this book, working with the individual aspects of your emotional fingerprint enables you to target problem areas and create change as well as to build on your strong points and preserve strength.

As I interviewed more and more people, however, I began to realize that the aspects of importance in each group do fall into five distinct patterns. The name of each is given here, followed by a description and the list of its aspects of importance.

Director: A director enjoys a good challenge, loves to feel free and independent, is a performer, has a purpose for what he or she does, and enjoys experiencing life. Directors are orchestrators and collaborators. They can take a diverse amount of information and process it into understandable knowledge for a large audience. They are great in social settings, bringing a variety of people together and making something happen. They find joy in overcoming obstacles and making a difference in the world. These aspects of importance fit into this category:

Confident in my appearance
Overcoming challenges

Free and independent
Being creative
Achieving my life's purpose
Performing
Experiencing life

Relator: A relator values building strong, long-term, healthy relationships. Relationships make these people feel important, because relators derive energy and security from their relationships. In the workplace, the strength of relators is in networking and inspiring other people to reach a higher level of productivity and accountability. Relators have a hard time being productive in any area if their personal relationships are in trouble. They are very loyal, and they will sacrifice a great deal to make sure that their relationships continue to grow. These aspects of importance fit into this category:

Connected to God, spirit, or the universe
In a loving relationship
Being a friend
Connected to family
In a position of influence
Being a good parent
Serving

Intellectual: An intellectual is stimulated through books, speeches, research, and other types of reading. Intellectuals often feel close to nature, and they tend to be highly organized. They feel successful when accomplishing a task. They are motivated to learn and grow. They would rather be learning something new than just sitting around. They want to better themselves and become more useful. They are driven to understand and to become more knowledgeable. These aspects of importance fit into this category:

Organized
In the moment

Relying on my knowledge
Healthy
Connected to nature
Learning
Honoring my standards

Validator: A validator feels loved when he or she is trusted, respected, praised, accepted, or needed. Validators enjoy being social and in relationships in which they are being validated. They are often very good at giving validation to others. They do not like to be ignored. They are offended when people they care about disrespect them. Their confidence stems from the strength of their relationships. If they believe that they are in healthy, caring, and trusting relationships, they feel strong, secure, and loved. These aspects of importance fit into this category:

Trusted
Given respect
Receiving praise
Receiving recognition
Validated
Needed
Accepted

Executive: An executive hates having nothing to do. Executives are productive and thrive on getting the job done. They are task-oriented and focused on getting results. They hate small talk and prefer tackling a project to sitting around wasting time. They are good at managing things. They feel productive when they are in control, solving problems, working, providing, and winning. They are happiest when they are pursuing or achieving a desired goal. These aspects of importance fit into this category:

In control
Providing
Working
Secure

Solving problems
Reaching my goals
Winning

In the table on page 37, identify your emotional fingerprint by selecting only one word from each group that makes you feel important. Total them at the bottom of the grid. The more words you have circled in a particular category of the D.R.I.V.E. System the more dominant that category is to your personality. Then read the corresponding definitions to see if it gives clarity to why you do what you do.

I encourage you to identify how many aspects of your emotional fingerprint fall into each type. If you have three or more aspects in one category, that's your dominant type. It's the part of your emotional fingerprint that shows up most often, or predominantly.

If two aspects of your emotional fingerprint fit into one category, that's a strong secondary category. It might influence your dominant category or take turns with it. For example, you might consistently be an executive with a strong director influence, or you might be an executive at work but a director in your personal life.

Even if you have only one aspect of importance in a particular category, it is part of your emotional fingerprint, and the type it belongs to is at least one characteristic of your personality.

Finally, as you read the types, think about people you know. Can you see them fitting into one type or another? Does that give you some clues about how to better communicate with them?

These types are a shortcut, an overall snapshot of your emotional fingerprint that can help you to understand quickly how you respond to people and situations. This can also help you to understand another person's responses. What will be more useful to you than the types, however, is the individual aspects of importance that make up your emotional fingerprint. As we'll see throughout this book, the more aware you are of each aspect of your emotional fingerprint, the more effective and the happier you will be.

D.R.I.V.E. System

	Director	**R**elator	**I**ntellectual	**V**alidator	**E**xecutive
Group 1	Appearance	God	Organization	Trust	Control
Group 2	Overcoming	Relationships	Moment	Respect	Providing
Group 3	Independence	Friends	Knowledge	Receiving praise	Work
Group 4	Creativity	Family	Health	Recognition	Security
Group 5	Life's purpose	Influence	Nature	Validation	Solving problems
Group 6	Performing	Good parent	Learning	Being needed	Goals
Group 7	Experience life	Service	Standards	Accepted	Winning
Total					

How Your Emotional Fingerprint Is Created

My clients often wonder whether their emotional fingerprints are ever likely to change. The answer is a qualified yes. Your emotional fingerprint *can* change, but only in response to a dramatic (extremely positive) or traumatic (extremely negative) event; it won't change on a daily or a weekly basis. You need a pivotal experience to create what I call a *mind shift*.

Dramatic events that create a mind shift include getting married; graduating from school; landing your first job; being accepted by friends, family, or a new love; shooting a winning shot seconds before the buzzer; or holding your child for the first time. In your childhood—when your emotional fingerprint is created—dramatic events can include being picked first for the basketball team, having a cute boy or girl want to sit next to you at lunch, getting a 100 on a test you studied for, being recognized by an adult, or being complimented on your appearance. Each of these positive mind shifts makes you feel unusually important, which makes them more significant than most everyday experiences.

Traumatic events cause you to feel unusually unimportant, which creates a deep inner desire to feel important instead. Such events include getting fired, being rejected by someone you like, or losing something precious. In your childhood, traumatic events can include being picked last for a game at recess, getting a bad grade, having someone make fun of you, having a teacher or another adult figure call you stupid or make you feel inferior, or trying really hard to do something and failing publicly.

My dear friend Tony Magee experienced a traumatic event in his childhood that created an aspect of his emotional fingerprint. Tony grew up in the Watts housing projects of East Los Angeles, where he was surrounded by violence, drugs, and gangs. He witnessed his first homicide at age four, when he saw a young man gunned down right in front of him.

While Tony was in first grade, he had an experience that may seem trivial to some people but that changed his life. One day his class was given an assignment to color pictures of fruits, and Tony was told to color a banana. I'll let him tell the rest of the story:

> I was so proud of the way I was coloring my banana. After everyone was finished, it was time for show-and-tell. So I showed my paper to the class, and everyone started to laugh. My teacher, Miss Pierce, was curious and said, "Let me see your paper." And she just fell out laughing, which gave permission to the whole class to laugh at me. And I'm wondering, "What are you guys laughing at? What's so funny?"
>
> She looked at my paper again, and she said, "Tony, you colored your bananas brown. Everyone knows that bananas are yellow."
>
> What Miss Pierce failed to realize was that when bananas are picked wherever they grow them—I've never seen a banana farm, okay? I mean, whether they grow them in Hawaii or Columbia, it sure wasn't Watts, okay?—they pick them, almost like Kelly green, like fresh new money, right? But by the time they make it to my neighborhood,

these bananas are essentially brown with little yellow spots. What was I to do? So when I colored my bananas, I colored them brown because that's all I knew. When my mother went to the store, they might have been a little yellow, but by the time she made it home, they were brown when I saw them.

So when everybody laughed at me, like a little turtle I just went into my shell. I was so sad I didn't talk to anybody for the rest of the day. I don't think I talked to anybody for the rest of the week. I was just so sad.

Tony experienced a traumatic event, and part of his emotional fingerprint was formed. Suddenly, an aspect of importance, relying on his knowledge, was set on fire. Never again would he allow himself to feel stupid. He went on to become the first person in his family to graduate from high school. Then he put himself through college. Eventually he became the first African American to work with NASA in metallurgy, designing rockets for the space shuttle. He had come a long way from the Watts housing project. He transformed the trauma of that experience into a positive way of feeling important. From that day forward, Tony's reliance on his knowledge made Tony feel important. A whole new life was the result.

You learn a lot about Tony when you understand that relying on his knowledge is part of his emotional fingerprint. Imagine if you knew the emotional fingerprints of your spouse or romantic partner, siblings, parents, teenagers, best friend, and favorite coworkers. Think how much better you would understand why they do what they do, how they have gotten to where they are in life, and what really moves them.

I highly recommend that you urge those close to you to fill in the "Determine Your Emotional Fingerprint" questionnaire. Of all the people I have interviewed, I've never found anyone who didn't want to discover his or her emotional fingerprint. After all, our favorite conversations are usually the ones about us. You'll find that people will often open up much more than you anticipate.

Just asking another person about what makes him or her feel important will have a surprisingly powerful effect on just about any conversation.

Now that you've identified the seven aspects of your emotional fingerprint, you're already able to live more consciously and make more effective choices. There are even more benefits awaiting you from becoming aware of your emotional fingerprint. Your next step is to learn how to master your emotional highs and lows.

2

Master Your Emotional Highs and Lows

I know of no more encouraging fact than the unquestionable ability of man to elevate his life by conscious endeavor.

—Henry David Thoreau

Lacey's phone was ringing off the hook. Clients had been calling since early that morning. Her boss had just come in and dumped a whole new load of work on her desk. Her son had called a few minutes ago to tell her that he hadn't made the first string of the school soccer team, as he'd been hoping for, and her husband had been worried for weeks about being laid off from his job.

Needless to say, Lacey was having a bad day. When her aunt Gina called, Lacey wasn't in the mood to talk to her, but her aunt had just had a biopsy for a suspected cancer, and Lacey wanted to hear the results. She was relieved to hear that the results were negative and that her favorite aunt was fine. Lacey even became a little tearful when she heard the good news, but after she got off the phone, her mind went back to racing like a hamster on a wheel in a cage. How was she going to get all this work done? How would she help her son recover from his disappointment? If her husband did get laid off, what would they do? Her salary would cover the mortgage, thank heavens, but what about their health insurance, the credit card bills, and . . .

Lacey's anxiety was interrupted by a knock on the wall of her cubicle. It was Meryl, a new coworker whom Lacey had only met last week.

"I won't keep you," Meryl said. "I just wanted to thank you so much for the recipe you gave me last week—for the cheese dip, remember? I made it for my husband's Super Bowl party just like you suggested, and it worked out perfectly. You really saved my life! The only problem is, they're all coming back next week to watch the hockey game, and I have *no* idea what to give them this time."

"Oh, I know just what you should serve," Lacey said, and promised to e-mail Meryl another recipe.

At first, Lacey was annoyed to have to give Meryl even a little bit of her attention, especially for such a trivial problem. After Meryl left, however, Lacey suddenly felt much better. She could imagine finishing the work that had seemed so daunting only a few minutes before, she felt sure she could comfort her son and help him to use his setback as a learning experience, and for some reason she just wasn't as worried about her husband losing his job. "I hope he won't, but if he does, we'll deal with it," she thought, and then she went back to work.

What just happened? Why did Lacey's genuine relief over her beloved aunt barely change her mood, but her brief conversation with Meryl, a person whom she barely knew, calm her anxiety and lift her spirits? Lacey had just experienced an emotional high, and she had just felt the power of her emotional fingerprint.

Understanding Your Emotional Highs and Lows

Emotional highs and lows can be very powerful—so powerful that sometimes they seem to run our lives. We can learn to control them, and in a few moments I'll tell you how. First, however, I want you to see for yourself how quickly a positive or negative mood swing can affect your life. Consider the following situations and see if they have happened to you:

- You're having the best day ever. Suddenly the phone rings, and you get bad news. Now you feel miserable, and all traces of your good mood are gone,
- You're down in the dumps, really feeling blue. Suddenly you get incredible news or something amazing happens, and you feel as though your whole world has changed. You can barely remember how low you felt just a few minutes before.
- You're at work, having an average day, when a coworker or your boss acknowledges you for doing a good job. Now you feel valued and important, glowing with contentment.
- You've made a sale or closed a deal at work, and you're feeling pretty good about things. Then you discover that your client has backed out. Now you feel thoroughly frustrated, angry, or upset.
- You've spent all morning cleaning your house, and you're quietly proud of how great everything looks. Then your family comes back. and no one says a word about all your hard work. Suddenly you're down in the dumps.

Do any of these experiences sound familiar? Emotions are powerful. Left unchecked, they can rule your life, pulling you around like a puppet on a string. It doesn't have to be that way, however. As you come to understand your emotional fingerprint, you'll learn how to master the process that causes your emotions to go up or down. You'll have the power to choose more positive, uplifting experiences and to begin to take control of your life.

When You're Feeling High

To feel this power for yourself, let's try another set of questions. As you complete the following exercise, look at the list of the seven aspects of your emotional fingerprint that you've written down.

Understanding Your Emotional Highs

1. A Positive Experience

Think of a time when you felt on top of the world. We all have our good days and our bad days, but I'm talking about a day when you just felt incredible, either because of a single event or in response to a whole chain of events. Write about the experience. The more details you can remember, the better.

_____

_____

_____

_____

_____

Now write down the seven aspects of importance of your emotional fingerprint. Put a checkmark beside any aspect that was validated during your positive experience.

1. _____

2. _____

3. _____

4. _____

5. _____

6. _____

7. _____

Add up the number of aspects of importance that were validated:

_____

2. Your Ideal Day

Imagine that you can wave a wand and create the best possible day of your life. What would that day be like? Visualize it in great detail. What would you be doing? Where would that day take place? In a resort? On a magnificent mountain? At your childhood home? Who would be part of it: spouse, kids, friends, other family members? Or would you be alone for all or part of your day? Would work be part of your day? Would your hobbies be included? The more details you can imagine, the better. Remember, this is a magic day, so it can start anywhere, end anywhere, and include anything and anyone you like. Describe that day—in full sentences or just rough notes.

_____

_____

_____

_____

_____

_____

Now write down the seven aspects of importance of your emotional fingerprint. Put a checkmark beside any aspect that was validated during your positive experience.

1. _____

2. _____

3. _____

4. _____

5. _____

6. _____

7. _____

Add up the number of aspects of importance that were validated:

_____

3. Scenes from Your Life

Think of your best friend and some of the amazing experiences you have had together over the years. Then look at your list of aspects of importance. Write down the aspects that are generally validated when you are with your friend.

_____

_____

Now count the aspects of importance and write down the total:

_____

Think of your spouse or romantic partner, especially when things are going great in your relationship and you feel love and appreciation from and for that person. Then look at your list of aspects of importance. Write down the aspects that are generally validated in the best times of your relationship.

_____

_____

Now count the aspects of importance and write down the total:

_____

What do you consider to be your greatest accomplishment?

_____

_____

Look at your list of aspects of importance. Write down the aspects that were validated while you were achieving that accomplishment.

_____

_____

Now count the aspects of importance and write down the total:

_____

By now you have probably noticed the pattern: great experiences validate your aspects of importance. Look back at your answers. Do you see that as you described each of your positive experiences, two or more aspects of importance were always being validated? In fact, that is the first principle of your emotional highs and lows.

Principle 1: When two or more aspects of your emotional fingerprint are validated, your mood improves.

Now you understand Lacey's experience. Although she loved her aunt dearly, even hearing good news about her aunt wasn't enough to break through Lacey's anxiety and despair. That's because the news of Aunt Gina didn't happen to validate Lacey's emotional fingerprint:

1. Being in control
2. Overcoming challenges
3. Receiving praise
4. Receiving recognition
5. Solving problems
6. Reaching goals
7. Serving

Lacey was glad to hear that her aunt was all right, but it wasn't enough to turn her day around.

On the other hand, Meryl, a far less important person in Lacey's life, did validate two of Lacey's aspects of importance. As we just saw, Lacey feels important when she's solving problems and serving, and Meryl gave Lacey a chance to do both. Principle 1 shows us that no matter what else is going on, validating two or more of your aspects of importance improves your mood.

In fact, validating two or more aspects of importance of your emotional fingerprint makes you feel successful, happy, joyful, and complete. More aspects that are being validated in a situation will create a greater sense of happiness and fulfillment. Your greatest moments in your life have been when five, six, or even all seven aspects of your emotional fingerprint have been met. The key to remember is it takes two simultaneously being validated to change your mood in a positive direction. Embracing this concept can revolutionize your personal life, relationships, and career. No longer do you have to be at the mercy of mood swings. If you feel down, turn it around: consciously and actively meet two or more aspects of your emotional fingerprint every day. Understanding your emotional highs and lows puts you in charge of your life. You alone know what you need to create an emotional high, putting you on top of the world.

When You're Feeling Low

Unfortunately, we don't experience only emotional highs. We also experience emotional lows. This brings us to the second principle of the emotional fingerprint.

> Principle 2: When two or more aspects of your emotional fingerprint are being disrespected, your mood gets worse.

This is when we have our emotional drops. It is when we feel frustrated, exhausted, or depressed. Your emotional fingerprint is disrespected when someone or something outside your control violates two or more of your aspects of importance. The longer your emotional fingerprint is disrespected, the deeper the negative side effects are.

For example, if you have an aspect of importance of being given respect or feeling accepted, and someone is rude to you, this might make you feel as though your emotional fingerprint has been disrespected. If you have an aspect of importance of being free and independent, and your boss informs you that you are now required to work weekends even though you never agreed to do so, or if your wife announces that her elderly father is coming for an extended visit and you have no choice but to take care of him, your emotional fingerprint may have been disrespected.

If you have the aspect of importance of being a good parent, and your in-laws or your friends tell you how to raise your children, you might experience them as disrespecting your emotional fingerprint. You might even disrespect your emotional fingerprint yourself through self-destructive behavior, such as pornography, drugs, or alcohol abuse, which might conflict with such aspects of importance as being in control, living in the moment, being free and independent, remaining healthy, achieving your life's purpose, reaching your goals, or honoring your standards.

My client Susan, a forty-three-year-old yoga trainer, had a frustrating experience in which her emotional fingerprint was disrespected. Exhausted and sweaty, she came home from a strenuous training session at the gym only to find that the house was a mess, the kids hadn't done their homework, and no one would help her make dinner. Her husband had worked late, and she felt totally alone in a house full of people. For some individuals, this wouldn't be a big deal, but because Susan's emotional fingerprint was being offended, it felt horrible to her.

Following is Susan's emotional fingerprint. Can you see which aspects of importance were being disrespected?

1. Being confident in my appearance
2. Living in the moment
3. Being free and independent
4. Being creative
5. Feeling validated
6. Achieving my goals
7. Winning

Susan validated many of her aspects of importance in her work as a trainer. There she felt confident in her appearance, in the moment, free and independent, creative, validated, and as though she were reaching her goals. She was, therefore, winning—not in the sense of surpassing other people in a contest but in the sense of having the life she wanted.

Nevertheless, as soon as Susan walked through the door of her house, her emotional fingerprint was instantly disrespected. Because her husband was working, she didn't feel free and independent—instead, she felt obligated to take care of the entire household by herself. Being left alone with all of the housework left Susan feeling like the opposite of being validated, and because those two aspects of importance were offended, she lost her ability to remain in the moment. Taking care of the kids and coping with a messy house didn't feel very creative, and in her frustration, Susan—who had been perfectly happy with her appearance when she left the gym—began to feel messy and unkempt. She had the despairing feeling that we all sometimes get of doubting that she would ever reach her goals, and she certainly didn't feel like a winner. What had started out as a good day quickly unraveled to become a miserable one.

In Susan's case, all seven aspects of her emotional fingerprint were being disrespected, but as the second principle asserts, disrespecing only two is enough to bring you down. The more aspects of your emotional fingerprint that are disrespected, the further down you go. Fortunately, the opposite is true as well: the more aspects of your emotional fingerprint that are validated, the happier you feel.

Let's take a closer look at how disrespecting the aspects of your emotional fingerprint affects *you*. Complete the following questionnaire.

QUESTIONNAIRE

Understanding Your Emotional Lows

- Who is the one person whose name you do not want to appear on your caller ID? _____

    Which aspects of importance of your emotional fingerprint does this person disrespect?

    _____

    _____

    How many aspects does this person disrespect? _____

- Name a person whom you can't stand to be around. _____
    Which aspects of your emotional fingerprint does this person disrespect?

    _____

    _____

    How many aspects does this person disrespect? _____

- Think of a recent instance in which you really felt the weight of the world on your shoulders. We all have our good days and bad days, but I am talking about a really depressing moment, frustrating situation, or a nothing-is-going-your-way day. It could involve a single incident or a whole chain of events. Describe that time, giving as many details as you can.

    _____

    _____

_____

_____

_____

Which aspects of importance of your emotional fingerprint did that experience disrespect?

_____

_____

How many aspects were offended? _____

As you can see, disrespecting your emotional fingerprint creates an emotional low as surely as validating your emotional fingerprint creates an emotional high. Once you're conscious of what offends your individual aspects of importance and what validates them—and once you see how greatly this offense or validation affects your mood—you're able to take far more control over your life and, ultimately, to own it. _You_ can control how you're going to feel, simply by making sure that at least two or more aspects of your emotional fingerprint are validated, and you can also respond more quickly and effectively when something happens that disrespects any part of your emotional fingerprint and brings you down. Mastering your emotional highs and lows is therefore a powerful way of learning how to own your life.

Taking Charge of Your Emotional Highs and Lows

It is challenging to hit a target you can't see. How can we expect to master our emotional highs and lows if we don't understand what creates them? Think of an elevator, which has buttons that correspond to certain floors. If you want to go to the twenty-third floor, you don't press the eleventh-floor button. Likewise, in our lives, we have buttons that when pushed immediately lead to particular emotions.

Think about it for a moment. Which buttons, when pushed, drive you completely crazy, frustrate you, or exhaust you? Which buttons, when pushed, make you feel loved, appreciated, and accepted?

Now imagine how powerful you'll become when you learn how to push the positive buttons while keeping the negative ones from being pushed. Complete the following questionnaire to identify your main "buttons."

QUESTIONNAIRE

Identifying Your Emotional "Buttons"

Think about the top five things that drag you down and the top five things that lift you up. Here's what pushes *my* emotional buttons. Your answers will be your own.

What typically drags me down?

1. People complaining about life
2. Someone changing my schedule
3. Too many things on my to-do list
4. Dealing with administrative work
5. Being trapped indoors all day

What usually lifts me up?

1. Spending time with my family
2. Painting, drawing, doing anything creative
3. Going to theme parks
4. Coaching and speaking
5. Being outside

What typically drags you down?

1. _____
2. _____
3. _____
4. _____
5. _____

What usually lifts you up?

1. _____
2. _____
3. _____
4. _____
5. _____

Discover Your Untapped Power

By listing your top five emotional ups and downs, you've taken a significant step toward taking control of your life. Knowing what lifts you up and what drags you down gives you the power to change your emotional life, because you can always learn to tap into the things that lift you up while watching for and avoiding the things that bring you down.

To understand more about your untapped power—your hidden ability to control your emotional life—you need to master three concepts:

1. What you focus on, you feel.
2. What you visualize, you internalize.
3. What you think about comes about.

Let's take a closer look at each of these concepts.

What You Focus on, You Feel

When Lacey was thinking about how swamped she was at work, her son not making it onto the soccer team, and her husband's likelihood of losing his job, she felt the results of her emotional fingerprint being disrespected. Focusing on these negative events made them larger and more important, until all Lacey could feel was anxiety, depression, and despair.

Whenever you focus on the problems in your life, you feel sad, angry, or anxious. As you imagine everything that might go wrong or how things could get even worse, it's as though your mind were staging a dress rehearsal for your actions. Just thinking about your emotional fingerprint being disrespected makes you actually feel disrespected, which in turn creates a new emotional low.

In contrast, when you focus on what is possible, feel gratitude for every blessing in your life, and are at peace with where you are, you feel optimistic, encouraged, and hopeful. Even if you're having a terrible day or facing a series of crises—a loved one's illness, a spouse's job loss—you begin to create an emotional high. Guard your thoughts, and your emotions will follow. Focus on the positive, and your emotions will respond in the affirmative. Focus on your blessings and on all the good in your life, and you will feel a crashing emotional low stop its downward trend as your mood starts to climb again.

As you focus on ways to validate your emotional fingerprint, you will be pushing the proper buttons to raise your spirits. If by chance someone has gained access to your emotional fingerprint and is pushing all the wrong buttons, distance yourself from that person—at least temporarily—and start focusing on validating at least one aspect of importance of your emotional fingerprint. You are in control of your emotional highs and lows—and of your life. No one can take that control away from you unless you let them.

What You Visualize, You Internalize

As Lacey started to visualize all of the terrible outcomes she was imagining—her son's distress, her husband's job loss, her own inability to meet her deadline—she felt terrible. When she started thinking about what recipe she was going to send to Meryl, she felt much better. That's because she felt good about being able to solve Meryl's problem, and she could imagine Meryl affirming that once again Lacey had succeeded. Visualizing this positive outcome—even though it hadn't actually happened yet—turned Lacey's mood around. Whether we visualize our problems or our successes, the result is the same: we internalize what we imagine, and we begin to experience the emotions that go with it.

We have all visualized something bad happening to us. When you're backing out of your driveway, for example, you might suddenly imagine that someone is behind your car. Your heart begins to race, and you swing around to make sure no one is there. Although the driveway is empty, you have lived through a mini disaster in your mind, imagining that you have hurt, perhaps killed, someone. Your palms sweat, your breathing grows rapid, and your stomach clenches—all of the things you would have felt if you had actually hit someone. No one was anywhere near the driveway, and you have done nothing wrong, but your entire body and all of your emotions are behaving as though you have. Visualizing a potential tragedy makes it real to you—almost as real as if it had actually happened.

Dr. Maxwell Maltz has said, "Experimental and clinical psychologists have proven beyond a shadow of a doubt that the human nervous system cannot tell the difference between an actual experience and an experience imagined vividly and in detail." This means that if you spend a lot of time imagining the worst, your body, your mind, and your spirit all feel the effects of that stress just about as much as if you had actually gone through those experiences—even if they never happen!

If you visualize a loved one leaving you or being disappointed in you, you internalize the emotions of fear, anxiety, and doubt. If you visualize a loved one being happy with you or doing something nice for you, your spirits lift immediately, almost as though he or she really did do whatever you imagined. Visualizing either a positive or a negative outcome creates the emotion appropriate to that outcome, even though it hasn't actually happened—and may never happen.

Some of the most significant research ever conducted on the power of visualization was published in 1958 by L. Verdelle Clark in his thesis for Wayne State University. One account of Clark's research reads as follows:

> At the University of Chicago a study was conducted to determine the effects of visualization on the free-throw performance of basketball players. First, the athletes were tested to determine their free-throw proficiency. They were then randomly assigned to one of three experimental groups. The first went to the gym every day for one hour and practiced throwing free throws. The second [group] also went to the gym, but instead of physically practicing, they lay down and simply visualized themselves successfully shooting. The third group did nothing. In fact, they were instructed to forget about basketball: "Don't touch a basketball—don't even think about it!" At the end of 30 days, the three groups were again tested to determine their free-throw proficiency.
>
> The players who hadn't practiced at all showed no improvement in performance; many in that group actually

exhibited a drop. Those who had physically practiced one hour each day showed a performance increase of 24 percent. Here's the clincher: the visualization group, by merely imagining themselves successfully shooting free throws, improved 23 percent!

So which do you want to imagine: yourself failing or yourself succeeding? Although you can't necessarily choose what happens to you in life, you can certainly choose what you *imagine* happening to you. Why not set yourself up for success—not to mention confidence and optimism—by imagining the best instead of the worst? Learning how to visualize the best is a skill like any other: it must be practiced, but it can be learned. Start practicing your ability to visualize the outcomes you want. You might be amazed at the results.

What You Think About Comes About

No action was ever performed without thought. Thoughts help to create the actions we take—and they also create the emotions we feel. Lacey felt better when she had new thoughts: that she could comfort her son and help him to use his setback as a learning experience; that her husband might not lose his job; that if he did, they would deal with it. We are where we are because of the thoughts we have had, and by having more positive thoughts, Lacey put herself in a more positive emotional state. Self-help author James Allen, in his epic masterpiece, *As a Man Thinketh*, put it very well when he said, "Let a man radically alter his thoughts, and he will be astonished at the rapid transformation it will effect in the material conditions of his life. Men imagine that thought can be kept secret, but it cannot; it rapidly crystallizes into habit, and habit solidifies into circumstances."

Allen wrote at a time when many authors used *man* to mean "people," but what he wrote is, of course, equally true for women. We can change our thoughts, letting go of pondering the negative aspects of our lives and thinking instead about what is working and what is right with our lives. We can also remind ourselves that we have the ability to make conscious decisions to switch our thoughts, focus on the positive, visualize good outcomes, and think about the results we want. The more we work on controlling our thoughts, the more empowered we will feel. We can use that power to do whatever it takes to validate two or more aspects of importance of our emotional fingerprints.

EXERCISE

Focus, Visualize, Think

1. Wherever you are—at home, at work, in a bookstore browsing through this book—look around and find something you consider ugly or unpleasant. It could be a dust bunny on the floor, a piece of office furniture you've always hated, or a crying child in the store—anything you find annoying or ugly. Take a minute or two to allow yourself to be conscious of all of the negative thoughts this unpleasant item engenders in you, particularly negative thoughts about yourself: "I don't like that. It's ugly. Why doesn't anybody see it but me? I hope nobody sees it but me! If I wasn't so lazy, I would have vacuumed and it wouldn't be here. I'm all alone here. I must be so selfish, because I just want that kid to stop crying!"

2. Now focus on something beautiful for one or two minutes. It could be as small as a little patch of color, a child's smile, or the way the books are stacked in the store. Focus as intently on the beautiful thing as you did on the ugly thing. Allow yourself to be conscious of all of the positive thoughts this pleasant object engenders in you, particularly positive thoughts about yourself: "I like that so much. I feel hopeful! I'm glad I brought such a beautiful thing into my space. I feel good seeing that kid smile. That really makes me happy."

Your experience validates the concepts we've just demonstrated:

What you focus on, you feel.

What you visualize, you internalize.

What you think about comes about.

Now you know the secret to mastering your emotional highs and lows. You simply have to make sure that at least two aspects of your emotional fingerprint are validated and that none of your emotional fingerprint is disrespected. At the same time, you can focus on the positive in your environment, your thoughts, and your feelings. You'll learn more about how to do this in part 2, when we talk about how to internalize your emotional fingerprint. Meanwhile, you can begin working on the mastery of your emotional highs and lows.

Follow the Platinum Rule

Just as validating or disrespecting your emotional fingerprint affects your mood and well-being, so too does validating or disrespecting other people's emotional fingerprints affect how their day goes. As a result, understanding another person's emotional fingerprint can give you a number of ways to affect the people with whom you come in contact. Whether you're thinking of family, friends, clients, colleagues, or customers, you can enormously widen your influence and improve your relationships by validating someone's emotional fingerprint and improving his or her day.

To make the best use of your insights into other people, keep in mind a principle that Dr. Tony Alessandra calls the Platinum Rule, which he likes to contrast with the Golden Rule. Instead of doing unto others as you would have them do unto you, do unto them what *they* would like, based on *their* emotional fingerprints.

There are actually several such rules:

The Pewter Rule: Do unto them before they do it to you.

The Silver Rule: Do unto yourself as you would have others do unto you.

The Golden Rule: Do unto others as you would have them do unto you.

The Platinum Rule: Do unto others as they would have you do unto them.

My client Martin learned the Platinum Rule while dealing with his wife, Joanne. Because one aspect of importance of Martin's emotional fingerprint is being needed, he assumed that Joanne had the same aspect—or rather, because Martin had never heard of emotional fingerprints before he came to me, he assumed that Joanne experienced love in the same way that he did. When he wanted to make Joanne feel cherished and appreciated, he found a hundred little ways to show her how much he needed her.

The problem was that Joanne did not have feeling needed on her list of aspects of importance—but she did have being free and independent. Thus, every time Martin showed Joanne how much he needed her, he wasn't making her feel loved, he was making her feel trapped. When Joanne bristled or tried to stop Martin's expression of need, Martin assumed that he simply hadn't gotten through to her. He redoubled his efforts to make her feel needed, which of course only succeeded in making her feel more trapped. This in turn made Joanne pull away more, and so a vicious cycle was born.

When I explained the concept of the emotional fingerprint to Martin, his face lit up in recognition. Before I even had the chance to suggest that he think about his wife's emotional fingerprint, Martin got there first. "No wonder Joanne has been so upset with me lately!" he exclaimed. "I haven't been giving her what *she* needs. I've been giving her what *I* need."

Armed with this new knowledge, Martin changed tactics. Now, instead of trying to make Joanne feel needed, he affirmed her freedom and independence. He encouraged her to take time away from the house and the kids, he expressed his interest in separate activities, and he made it clear that while he loved her and was deeply committed to her, he also knew how to get along without her. Joanne so appreciated the new space in their relationship that she became much more affectionate and responsive—so Martin got to feel needed after all.

My client Sondra had a similar experience. She had been struggling with a prickly boss at her new job, a woman who seemed deeply threatened by Sondra's accomplishments and ability.

Sondra had tried to placate the woman by giving her respect, since Sondra herself felt important when she was given respect.

Sondra's boss, however, didn't have that particular aspect of importance. She felt important when she was providing. What she wanted to hear from Sondra was not how much Sondra respected her but rather how much good use Sondra was making of all of the help and knowledge that her boss was sharing with her. Sondra discovered that acknowledging her boss's providing went quite a long way toward smoothing their relationship.

If you don't know someone's emotional fingerprint, I suggest an approach that I call *paying attention to the obvious*. The president of my local bank wanted to make her employees feel important, but she didn't feel comfortable asking them about their emotional fingerprints. "How can I create emotional highs for them if I don't have that basic information about them?" she asked me.

Instead of answering, I gave her a living demonstration of paying attention to the obvious. I went up to one of the tellers, who had a little statue of the Eiffel Tower and pictures of herself around the world, and said, "Oh, I love the Eiffel Tower. Have you been there?"

"No," she replied, as she perked up, "but I am saving up to go. I have been to Greece, Germany, New York, and Australia."

"Do you love to travel?" I inquired.

"Oh, yes!" she replied. She told me where she and her husband had gone on their honeymoon, that she had almost taken a job as a flight attendant instead of working at the bank, and that she still had a dream of getting a pilot's license.

The president was shocked that I had discovered so much information about the teller. She said, "I have worked with that woman for eighteen months, and she never told me that she liked to travel or that she wanted to be a pilot."

I smiled and said, "You never asked."

People validate their emotional fingerprints by what they wear, what they hang on their walls or choose as a screen saver, what kind of cars they drive, where they live, how they decorate their homes and their offices, what groups they join, who is in their social circles, what people they spend their time with, what hobbies they have, what bumper stickers they display, what they put on their blogs or social networking sites, and what they say. All we have to do is pay attention, and we'll see what matters to them. Then we can follow the Platinum Rule.

If you have the chance, I always recommend asking someone to take the quiz in chapter 1 to identify his or her emotional fingerprint, but sometimes that just isn't possible. In that case, I suggest that you pay attention to the obvious and then follow the Platinum Rule. Commenting on the things you notice will naturally lift up someone's emotional elevator, and the person will feel important. Your relationship with him or her will immediately improve as a result. As the poet and novelist Maya Angelou has observed, "I've learned that people will forget what you said, people will forget what you did, but people will never forget how you made them feel."

EXERCISE

Paying Attention to the Obvious

1. Think of two people with whom you get along well and of whom you'd like to be more supportive. They can be anyone, from a spouse or another family member to a customer or a colleague. What things seem obviously important to them? Their hobbies? The way they decorate their homes? The trips they take? Their health routines? Perhaps the way they dress?

   Write down their names and list the obvious things that make them feel important. What three things could you talk about the next time you are on the phone with them or are face-to-face?

   _____

   _____

2. Next time you see these people, make a point of bringing up at least two of the items on your list. How did they respond? Did they seem happier when you left? Did they feel uplifted?

What would you say differently next time? Write about the experience.

_____

_____

Making the Other Person Feel Important

There is one all-important law of human conduct. If we obey that law, we shall almost never get into trouble. In fact, that law, if obeyed, will bring us countless friends and constant happiness. But the very instant we break the law, we shall get into endless trouble. The law is this: *Always make the other person feel important.*

–Dale Carnegie, *How to Enjoy Your Life and Your Job*

Dale Carnegie was the first person to alert me to the power of feeling important, so he was clearly aware of the need to make *others* feel important. I've suggested that you do that by learning or imagining the other person's emotional fingerprint or perhaps his or her type (see "Which Type Are You?" in chapter 1). You can also help someone to create an emotional high when you pay attention to the obvious. The final helpful approach is what I call the five validations.

I taught this approach to my client Peter, who works as a manager at a car dealership, and it revolutionized his business. Peter is a straightforward, no-nonsense, extremely logical man who was used to focusing on facts and figures, both with his customers and with his sales staff. Because Peter was the kind of man people instantly trusted—in fact, being trusted was a key aspect of importance of his emotional fingerprint—he did well enough, but he had come to me because he believed he was capable of more.

What Peter had to realize was that a straightforward, practical presentation was often not the best way to reach people. Sometimes people were interested in the practical details of the cars they were buying—as Peter himself would have been—but sometimes they were more interested in being validated. When Peter learned how to validate his customers—and his sales staff—everyone was happier. Sales increased, everybody made more money, and Peter had both financial and personal rewards from seeing his business flourish.

The five validations are a quick and easy way to make someone's emotional fingerprint feel validated even when you don't know what it is. Just about everyone wants recognition, respect, acceptance, appreciation, and praise, so if you make it a practice to shower people with these validations—sincerely, but deliberately—you'll make them feel important.

The next time you are with your friends or family members, use these five validations and see how they respond. The next time you are facing a conflict—whether with a casual acquaintance, a stranger, or a difficult person you know—try these five validations as well. If anything can smooth your path, these can.

Recognition. Successful entrepreneur Bill Bartmann told me in an interview that he was homeless at age fourteen, had dropped out of high school, and had joined a gang. When he was seventeen he worked in a hotel, and a woman in management kept calling him a "bright young kid." After a month or two of this, he inquired why. She said that this was what the owner of the hotel had put on his application after his interview. This recognition from someone he admired completely changed Bill's outlook on himself. It inspired him to get his GED, put himself through college and law school, and eventually build his own company into a billion-dollar empire. At one point he was ranked as one of the twenty-five richest people in America by *Forbes*. Bill told me that none of this would have happened if the owner of the hotel had not recognized him as a "bright young kid." The recognition you give can have a lasting impression on someone's emotional fingerprint. More immediately, it can create a warm and trusting relationship.

Respect. We all recognize respect as precious because it must be earned. Find something to respect in the people you know and let them know how highly you think of them. You might choose to express your respect for something as simple as their commitment to a workout routine or a hobby, or perhaps they have a talent or a capability that you respect. Ideally, you would express respect for their decisions and opinions, as well.

Mary Kay Ash was overlooked many times for promotions by her superiors. She was often the top salesperson in her corporate job and had amazing rapport with her customers, but somehow she was never respected by top management. In frustration she left the company she was working for and started Mary Kay Cosmetics. She later said, "No matter how busy you are, you must take time to make the other person feel important." She also told her sales force, "Pretend that every single person you meet has a sign around his or her neck that says, 'Make me feel important.' If you do this you will not only succeed in sales, you will succeed in life."

Mary Kay clearly understood the need for respect. Lack of respect caused her company to lose her talents. Her gift for respect created a multimillion-dollar business. We all need respect—so offer it to those whom you feel deserve it, and make sure they know how you feel.

Acceptance. Acceptance can be a challenge to those of us with strong judgments and opinions, but nothing is more powerful in making relationships go smoothly than a big dose of acceptance. When I have trouble accepting someone, I try to take a step back and gain a bit of perspective, often by thinking of the following story.

A little boy was telling his grandmother how "everything" was wrong with Dennis, the boy who sat behind him at school. Dennis made fun of him, Dennis wouldn't share his toys, Dennis bragged that he had a better lunch than anybody else, Dennis picked him last for the dodgeball team. The boy didn't have a good word to say about his classmate, and he complained to his grandmother that because of Dennis, he didn't even want to go to school anymore.

Meanwhile, Grandma was baking a cake. She promised her grandson a piece when it was ready, but meanwhile asked him if he wanted a snack, which of course he did.

"Here. Have some cooking oil," she said.

"Yuck," said the boy.

"How about a couple of raw eggs?"

"Gross, Grandma!"

"Would you like some flour, then? Or maybe baking soda?"

"Grandma, those are all yucky!"

Grandma replied, "Yes, all those things seem bad all by themselves. But when they are put together in the right way, they make a wonderfully delicious cake! And I'm sure that even though Dennis does all these very annoying things, we can still find a way to see him as a good kid."

As we accept people for who they are rather than objecting to their individual quirks, we will come to see that as a whole they are greater than their individual parts. Their basic humanity—even if they have done terrible things—is greater than any individual thing they have done. We may not like them, agree with them, or approve of them, but we can find a way to accept that—and that can improve a difficult relationship to a remarkable extent.

Appreciation. As Jeff Sinclair pulled his car up to the drive-through window at a fast-food restaurant, he asked the cashier what was owed by the car behind him. The cashier didn't understand why Jeff wanted to know, but she was soon stunned to realize that Jeff planned to pay for the people behind him as well as for his own order.

An hour later, Jeff's wife called and asked if he had been buying meals for people again.

"Yes, I have," Jeff answered. "What makes you ask?"

To Jeff's astonishment, a story had just been broadcast on the radio that the "paying it forward" practice (doing something nice for someone else after another person has done something nice for you) had been going on for fifty-three cars in a row. When Jeff told me about it, I asked him why he had paid for the other car in the first place.

"I just wanted to show appreciation for someone else," Jeff told me.

"But you didn't know the other people in the next car, did you?"

"No, I didn't," Jeff said. "But that doesn't mean I can't appreciate them."

Apparently, a lot of people felt the same way Jeff did, because the chain of "paying it forward" continued for another hour, until seventy-four people had shown their appreciation for complete strangers.

To me, this story makes it crystal clear that we live in an appreciation-deficient society. Imagine how your friends and loved ones would feel if they knew how much you appreciated them. Imagine how any relationship—from the serious to the casual—would improve with appreciation.

Praise. Master illusionist and magician Harry Houdini spent a lifetime debunking psychics, mind readers, and scam artists. He met every foe with enthusiasm, and within days he copied their tricks or proved them wrong. Magician and escape artist James Randi followed in the master's footsteps by offering a million dollars to anyone who could prove paranormal or psychic abilities. No one has ever claimed that money. So why do we think that our friends, families, coworkers, and customers know how we feel about them? Until they develop psychic abilities, I recommend that you praise them wholeheartedly and as often as you can. It is not enough to think positively about them. You must let them know how you feel.

Living Consciously

When you become aware of how your emotional fingerprint has affected your life, you develop insight into how to change future outcomes. No longer do you have to wonder why you are being hurt by someone's comments or their expectations of you. You can see immediately which aspect of importance of your emotional fingerprint is being disrespected by others' actions or remarks, and, more important, you can take conscious, effective steps to validate those aspects yourself. No longer do you have to wonder or be confused about why you have ups and downs. Instead, you can track your mood changes with a surgeon's precision, always understanding how your emotional fingerprint lifts you up or brings you down.

Understanding your emotional fingerprint puts you in the driver's seat of your own emotions. If you're having a bad day, you can consciously shift that day's direction by looking at your seven aspects of importance and then creating an environment or a situation in which two or more of them will be validated. You are aware of who you are, you understand how the outside world affects you, and you're able to take conscious, effective action as a result.

To truly understand how to live consciously, however, there is one more concept that you need to embrace: your emotional compass. That's what we'll look at next, in chapter 3.

3

Embrace Your Emotional Compass

Hamlet: Denmark's a prison.

. . .

Rosencrantz: We think not so, my lord.
Hamlet: Why then, 'tis none to you; for there is
nothing either good or bad, but thinking makes it
so: to me it is a prison.

—William Shakespeare, *Hamlet*, act 2, scene 4

When I was in school, the free and independent aspect of importance of my emotional fingerprint led me to avoid reading Shakespeare and pretty much anything that was assigned to me in English class. When I was older, I was astonished when I came upon the phrase "there is nothing either good or bad, but thinking makes it so." I could not imagine that five hundred years ago, William Shakespeare had articulated the principle of the emotional compass: the idea that each of us has his or her own ideas about what is good and what is bad and that our judgment about these things creates the experience of our lives.

Look at what is going on in this scene of *Hamlet*. Hamlet, the philosophy student, is forced to leave his university in Germany to return to the family home in Denmark. There he discovers that his beloved father has died, his mother has remarried, and the man she has married, his father's brother, may very well be the man who murdered Hamlet's father. Hamlet is supposed to remain in Denmark because that's what his mother has requested, but he suspects—correctly—that his uncle wants to maintain control over him.

The ghost of his father returns periodically, insisting that he was murdered and that young Hamlet take revenge by killing his uncle. Is the ghost real, or is he Hamlet's grief-induced hallucination? If Hamlet does kill his uncle, what will the rest of the kingdom think, especially if he can't prove that his uncle really *was* the murderer?

No wonder Hamlet thinks that Denmark is a prison! To him, freedom was being at school, where all he had to do was study abstract ideas. Even though his life in the royal family must look very glamorous from the outside, returning to his responsibilities as son, prince, and future king seems to him to be the ultimate imprisonment.

Hamlet is finally driven to kill his uncle, but the effort costs him his life and leads to the destruction of the entire kingdom. When I was a teenager in high school, I found the story boring. As an adult, however, it makes me appreciate just how far a person will go to validate his or her emotional fingerprint. In fact, Hamlet's story is a perfect illustration of the principle of the emotional compass, the third principle of the emotional fingerprint.

Principle 3: You will do anything within your belief system to defend or validate your emotional fingerprint.

Understanding Your Emotional Compass

Your emotional compass is the belief system that governs your behavior. It includes the big moral questions, such as killing, cheating, and committing adultery, but it also includes more mundane, everyday behaviors that reveal your emotional temperament: gossiping, fighting with a friend, being honest at work, loving your family, being a good friend, and being a productive employee.

For example, a man might love his children deeply, but it might not be within his belief system to say "I love you" or to hug and kiss his children, especially his sons. If such a man has the aspect of importance of being a good parent, he might lay down his life to protect his children or work long hours to send them to good schools. Nevertheless, it may not be within his belief system to let his young son sit on his lap, to play tag with him, or to put into words how much he loves the child. Even if someone showed this father volumes of psychology books arguing for another type of parenting, he still would not express his aspect of importance of being a good parent with hugs and warm words. He will restrict himself to the actions that are consistent with his own belief system about what it means to be a father and a man.

Shakespeare understood very well the power of the emotional compass when he wrote *Hamlet*. According to Hamlet's emotional compass, confirming that his uncle killed his father meant that Hamlet had to kill his uncle. If you and I found out something similar about a family member, our emotional compasses would probably demand a very different type of action. Even if we had the same emotional fingerprint as Hamlet's, we wouldn't necessarily take the same actions that he did, because our emotional compasses are different. In fact, even if you and I had identical emotional fingerprints, we would probably not express or interpret them in the same way, at least partly because of our different emotional compasses.

Understanding your emotional compass is the key to owning your life; it allows you to make conscious, clear, and focused decisions about how you express your emotional fingerprint. Perhaps you have the chance to take a job that pays well, has a lot of prestige, and supports your aspects of importance of being in control, providing, and being secure. Yet you object to something about the company. You know that it doesn't produce a good product, that it is not respectful of the environment, or that it doesn't deal honestly with its shareholders and investors. Perhaps working there would require you to show deference to a boss whom you simply don't respect, or you would have to adapt to a formal, stuffy corporate culture that just doesn't fit your personality.

You will do anything to validate your emotional fingerprint *within your belief system*—but something about working for that company just doesn't fit your belief system. With some regret, you pass on this apparently great job and continue to validate your emotional fingerprint in another way.

Suppose that your emotional fingerprint includes being given respect, being free and independent, and being creative. You have the chance to take the same job. You simply hate the idea of being treated disrespectfully by an arrogant boss, of being tied down to a rigid routine, and of giving up your creativity to work for someone else, but your own independent business has just gone under, you're aware of how bad the economy is, and you're responsible for supporting your children, your aged parents, and your unemployed brother. Now your belief system may not allow you to validate your emotional fingerprint by refusing the job and looking elsewhere. Your belief system may require you to take the job and validate your emotional fingerprint in another way.

Two different situations and two different decisions—in both cases, your emotional compass sets the limits for how you will and will not validate your emotional fingerprint.

Once you become conscious of your emotional compass, you might decide to change your belief system. Perhaps you'll realize that you've been too rigid, or maybe you'll decide that you've been too free and easy. Perhaps you'll loosen some of your fixed ideas and try out some new ways of acting and thinking—or maybe you'll become even more rigorous and demanding, calling on yourself to do a better job of living up to your beliefs. Either way, embracing your emotional compass can help you to make more satisfying and effective choices. Otherwise, you will be living at cross-purposes with yourself, telling yourself that you believe in one thing while actually believing in—and acting on—another.

Becoming Aware of Your Emotional Compass

Consider the aspects of importance of your emotional fingerprint. Write down something you would do and something you would not do to validate each of them.

To help you get started, here is my own emotional compass:

1. Being connected to God, spirit, or the universe

Something I would do to validate this aspect of my emotional fingerprint: I attend church, read scriptures, and teach my children gospel principles and to have hope and faith.

Something I would *not* do to validate this aspect of my emotional fingerprint: I would never push my beliefs on someone else. I would never try to prove that my theology is more correct than yours. I would never fail to believe in better times and better days.

2. Providing

Something I would do to validate this aspect of my emotional fingerprint: I am dedicated to my work. Even on vacations, my wife lets me work a couple of hours a day so I can stay sane. I love teaching our children about work. Since they were three years old, I have required my children to earn their own money for all of their toys.

Something I would *not* do to validate this aspect of my emotional fingerprint: I would never lie, cheat, or steal to get ahead. No matter how broke I become trying to make my dreams a reality, I would never give up being an entrepreneur and get a "real job." I would never work on Sunday.

3. Being free and independent

Something I would do to validate this aspect of my emotional fingerprint: I would do just about anything to validate this aspect of my emotional fingerprint. In my life I have done a lot of ridiculous things—including leaving good relationships, quitting well-paying jobs, and leaving school—because I thought that those actions were necessary to validate my freedom and independence.

Something I would *not* do to validate this aspect of my emotional fingerprint: I would not walk all over someone else's freedom or independence to validate my own. I would never hurt someone intentionally so that I could feel free and independent.

4. Being creative

Something I would do to validate this aspect of my emotional fingerprint: I would spend any amount of money to express my creativity in my work. I have self-funded movies, books, card systems, and games for my work. I would spend money on customizing a car with unusual tires, stereos, paint jobs, and engine modifications.

Something I would *not* do to validate this aspect of my emotional fingerprint: I would not spend a lot of money on household items for the sake of being creative. I would not use ideas from someone else without giving him or her due credit.

5. Achieving my life's purpose

Something I would do to validate this aspect of my emotional fingerprint: I would throw reason and common sense out the window to validate this aspect of my emotional fingerprint. There is no risk I would not take to get the message of this book out to the world. There have been countless times when I should have stopped or retreated, but to defend my life's purpose of getting this message out, I have pressed forward.

Something I would *not* do to validate this aspect of my emotional fingerprint: This is a challenging consideration. There is almost nothing I would not do, but my emotional compass does not allow me to risk my family to achieve my life's purpose. My belief that family comes first is simply too strong.

6. Being a good parent

Something I would do to validate this aspect of my emotional fingerprint: I would cancel any appointment when my kids need me to or when my wife needs me to in order to take care of the kids. I would postpone a business trip to attend a school play. I would sacrifice my free time and work late if my kids needed me during the day or if my wife needed me to help her be a good parent. All of these things I have done many times.

Something I would *not* do to validate this aspect of my emotional fingerprint: I would not let my kids walk over me or my wife. I would not spoil them or allow them to be lazy. When my kids are older, if they do something significantly wrong, I will not intervene; I will allow them to experience the consequences.

7. Experiencing life

Something I would do to validate this aspect of my emotional fingerprint: I would never allow my life to be ordinary. I prefer chaos to consistency, craziness to sanity. I want to experience it all: travel and home life, smiles and cries, the ups and the downs—everything this life has to offer.

Something I would *not* do to validate this aspect of my emotional fingerprint: I would never walk all over someone else to get what I want. I would never go into debt to experience life.

Now list your aspects of importance and the items for your emotional compass:

1. _____

    Something I would do to validate this aspect of my emotional fingerprint: _____

    _____

    Something I would *not* do to validate this aspect of my emotional fingerprint: _____

    _____

2. _____

    Something I would do to validate this aspect of my emotional fingerprint: _____

    _____

    Something I would *not* do to validate this aspect of my emotional fingerprint: _____

    _____

3. _____

    Something I would do to validate this aspect of my emotional fingerprint: _____

    _____

Something I would *not* do to validate this aspect of my emotional fingerprint: _____

_____

4. _____

Something I would do to validate this aspect of my emotional fingerprint: _____

_____

Something I would *not* do to validate this aspect of my emotional fingerprint: _____

_____

5. _____

Something I would do to validate this aspect of my emotional fingerprint: _____

_____

Something I would *not* do to validate this aspect of my emotional fingerprint: _____

_____

6. _____

Something I would do to validate this aspect of my emotional fingerprint: _____

_____

Something I would *not* do to validate this aspect of my emotional fingerprint: _____

_____

7. _____

Something I would do to validate this aspect of my emotional fingerprint: _____

_____

Something I would *not* do to validate this aspect of my emotional fingerprint: _____

_____

Now think of three things that you have seen other people do that you are certain you would never do. They might be moral issues, such as cheating or lying in certain types of situations; lifestyle issues, such as decisions about relationships, living situations, or types of dress; or emotional issues, such as what types of conversations you choose to have with a partner, how you relate to your family, or the way you handle work or your career. Write down the three things you would never do:

I would never

1. _____
_____

2. _____
_____

3. _____
_____

Look back at your answers in this exercise. Then complete the following sentences:

1. My emotional compass requires me to
_____
_____

2. My emotional compass will not allow me to
_____
_____

Think about everything you've written. How do you feel about your emotional compass? Are you proud of it? Frustrated by it? Ready to embrace it? Eager to change it?

_____
_____
_____
_____
_____

Validating Your Emotional Fingerprint: How Far Will You Go?

It never ceases to amaze me how far people will go to validate their emotional fingerprints. In *Hamlet*, as in many of Shakespeare's plays, characters are actually willing to defend their emotional fingerprints to the death, killing others or risking their lives to validate their need to be in control, be in a loving relationship, be a friend, or feel connected to family, to name a few. One of my favorite figures from U.S. history, Harriet Tubman, risked her life repeatedly: first to gain freedom for herself, then to bring her family and many others out of slavery.

To use an example that is closer to home: For the last years of his life, my father-in-law was severely incapacitated from chronic pain in both of his knees. He was heavyset, which made matters worse—so much so that he could barely walk. Every Tuesday night, however, he would muster up the strength to go bowling, despite the admonitions of his family and his friends. Why was this so important to him?

My father-in-law was quite good at bowling. In fact, of all the things he ever did in his life, bowling may have been the thing that he was best at. In his heyday, he actually broke a forty-two-year-old local record by shooting three consecutive three-hundred-point games. He was proud of his bowling success, which met his aspects of importance of being in control, receiving recognition, and winning.

Not only did bowling validate my father-in-law's emotional fingerprint, pushing himself hard to play for his league fit his emotional compass, which included the beliefs that a man doesn't give in to pain, pamper himself, or let down his team. So every Tuesday night, like clockwork, my father-in-law would drag himself out of bed and head for the bowling alley, suffering the intense pain and sacrificing potential healing, stability, and the future function of his knees just so he could bowl.

You might admire my wife's father, or you might think he was stubborn, self-destructive, or mistaken in his priorities. Perhaps you admire him *and* think those things. Yet what you think, what I thought, or what anyone in his family thought didn't matter to him or affect how he was going to validate his emotional fingerprint. All that mattered was what *he* thought, which was (though not in these words) that validating his emotional fingerprint within the behavior permitted—or perhaps demanded—by his emotional compass was more important than any other consideration.

Here's another example of the way the emotional compass sets the boundaries for what someone is and isn't able to do. My dear friend Tess has a lovely baby girl and a demanding job as a marketing consultant. She earns a good living, but as a result of her job and her baby—not to mention her husband—time is at a premium for her.

In spite of this, Tess has spent about ten hours a week for the last three years researching garage sales online. Although she can afford to shop anywhere, she prefers getting a good deal. She barters with everyone. When she goes to the drugstore, the mall, or any other store or market, she negotiates better prices. One day she bought a toy for three dollars. It didn't work the way she wanted it to, so she took it back to get a refund—from a *garage sale*! She rode her bike back to the garage sale, with her child riding in the bike carrier, which she had bought at another garage sale. The carrier tore as she was riding, so she pulled over and bought a pillow for two dollars for the child to sit on. As a result, Tess saved only one dollar by taking the toy back. Yet her emotional compass drove her to validate her emotional fingerprint this way.

When you understand your emotional fingerprint, you begin to understand why you make some of the choices you do that seem important or compelling to you even when they don't make much sense to the people around you. Consciously or subconsciously, you will do anything within your belief system to defend and support your emotional fingerprint. Use the following exercise to explore some of these choices.

EXERCISE

Learning More about Your Emotional Compass

Answer the following questions.

Personal Life

1. What hobbies, interests, or activities do you pursue to defend or support your emotional fingerprint?

Hobby, Interest, or Activity   Aspects Supported

_____   _____

_____   _____

_____   _____

2. What goals or ambitions are most important to you right now? How do they relate to your emotional fingerprint?

Goal or Ambition   Aspects Supported

_____   _____

_____   _____

_____   _____

3. What political or religious opinions or worldview do you hold to defend or support your emotional fingerprint?

Opinion   Aspects Supported

_____   _____

_____   _____

_____   _____

4. When was the last time you moved to a new residence? How did that defend or support your emotional fingerprint?

Move   Aspects Supported

_____   _____

_____   _____

_____   _____

5. What songs, quotations, sayings, or other material do you find supporting or uplifting? What aspects of your emotional fingerprint do they support?

Song, Quote, Saying, Other   Aspects Supported

_____   _____

_____   _____

_____   _____

Relationships

1. Are you in a romantic relationship now? If so, how does that relationship help you to support and defend your emotional finger-print? If you're not in a romantic relationship now but are looking for one, what aspects of your emotional fingerprint do you imagine supporting and defending when you are in your next relationship? How do you envision that happening? If you are not in a romantic relationship and are not looking for one, what aspects of your emotional fingerprint does that support or defend?

Romantic Relationship	Aspects Supported
_____	_____
_____	_____
_____	_____

2. Think of a recent argument or conflict that you had with someone. What aspects of your emotional fingerprint were you trying to defend or support?

Conflict	Aspects Supported
_____	_____
_____	_____
_____	_____

3. Who are your best friends, and what aspects of your emotional fingerprint do they support?

Friend	Aspects Supported
_____	_____
_____	_____
_____	_____

4. Do you get along with your parents? What aspects of your emotional fingerprint are validated or disrespected?

Mother	Aspects Validated or Disrespected
_____	_____
_____	_____
_____	_____

Father   Aspects Validated or Disrespected

_____   _____

_____   _____

_____   _____

5. Think of the last new friend you made or the person with whom you most recently felt a strong connection. What aspects of your emotional fingerprint does that person support?

New Connection   Aspects Supported

_____   _____

_____   _____

_____   _____

Business

1. Why did you take your job? What aspects of your emotional fingerprint were being supported?

Reasons for Taking Job   Aspects Supported

_____   _____

_____   _____

_____   _____

2. Think of the last time you voluntarily left a job. Did a new opportunity validate your emotional fingerprint, or did the old job so disrespect your emotional fingerprint that you had to leave?

Reasons for Leaving Job   Aspects Validated or Disrespected

_____   _____

_____   _____

_____   _____

3. Have you ever taken a job you didn't like to defend or support your emotional fingerprint? Identify your reasons for doing or not doing so and how that affected your emotional fingerprint.

Reasons for Taking or Not   Aspects Supported
Taking Undesirable Job

_____   _____

_____   _____

_____   _____

4. Describe your dream work situation, whether that is a job, a company you run, or a form of retirement. What aspects of your emotional fingerprint would that situation validate?

Dream Situation   Aspects Supported

_____   _____

_____   _____

_____   _____

We Don't All Have the Same "North Star"

I want to return to the quote from *Hamlet* that affected me so much the first time I read it: "There is nothing either good or bad, but thinking makes it so." What a powerful idea! Each of us is so used to assuming that our judgments about good and bad are self-evident "common sense" that we might have trouble acknowledging that other people's judgments are just as meaningful and obvious to them.

It's useful to remember that other people have their own points of view—visions of the truth that seem obvious to them. I'm not necessarily saying that you should question the accuracy of your own perspective. Consider the case of Wilbur Glenn Voliva, a millionaire in 1931 who was absolutely convinced that the earth was as flat as a pancake—circular, yes, but certainly not spherical. He believed—and was willing to challenge anyone who believed otherwise—that the center of the circular dish called earth was the North Pole and that the edges of the planet were surrounded by a vast wall of ice that the rest of the world mistakenly called the South Pole.

"We can praise God that this ice wall exists," Voliva once said. "It prevented Antarctic explorers like Sir James Ross from sailing right off the edge of the world. As for Magellan and others who claim to have circumnavigated the globe, they merely sailed all the way around the outside edge of the disc. It was an extraordinary achievement, but it did not prove the earth was round."

Like many of us, Voliva had confidence in the validity of his beliefs. "I can whip to smithereens any man in the world in a mental battle," he said. "I have never met any professor or student who knew as much on the subject as I do." Every year he ran an advertisement in the Chicago and Milwaukee newspapers offering five thousand dollars to anyone who could convince him that the world was not flat. No one ever could.

Voliva's story is unusual, but it's not unique. How many times have you tried to explain to somebody what he or she needed to do to change, but no matter what you said, no matter what evidence you submitted, you just could not get your message across? You could logically elucidate factual points until you were blue in the face, but if the other person was not willing to take action, nothing would change. It's not personal. It's just because we will do anything within our belief systems to defend and support our emotional fingerprints. Voliva's belief system was that the earth was flat.

As a society, we seem to have an equally limited perspective. Let's look at the example of the "war on terror." Nearly three thousand people needlessly lost their lives in the September 11, 2001, terrorist attacks. However, more than four hundred thousand Americans die every year because of cancer directly related to smoking. So how should we prioritize the war on terrorism, in terms of resources? I am certainly not making light of those whose lives were sacrificed during 9/11, or the brave men and women who defend our country. Consider it this way, however: If a terrorist came into the United States and blew up four hundred thousand people every year consistently for decades, would we not use all of our military and other resources to stop it? Why does the one cause get more money than the other, especially in light of the number of lives lost to the latter cause? It is an interesting quandary.

Here's one solution that might realign our resources. Subtract $173 billion from the defense budget (roughly 25 percent). That's what it would cost to buy all of the shares in the five largest tobacco companies, which account for 97 percent of all tobacco sold. Close those companies' doors and then make it illegal to buy, sell, or trade tobacco.

That would be a bold, decisive, and probably unpopular action. However, it might be more effective in actually saving the most human lives. After all, the U.S. defense budget in 2010 was $658 billion. In 2006, it was $515 billion—more than the combined defense budgets of China, Russia, Britain, France, Japan, Germany, Saudi Arabia, South Korea, India, Brazil, Australia, Canada, Indonesia, and the Netherlands. The U.S. defense budget is nine times larger than the defense budget of China, the next biggest defense spender.

These statistics are shocking, considering that the fourteen countries we outspend account for 60 percent of the world's population, whereas the United States accounts for only 5 percent. U.S. Secretary of Defense Robert Gates has said, "As much as the U.S. Navy has shrunk since the end of the Cold War, for example, in terms of tonnage, its battle fleet is still larger than the next 13 navies combined—and 11 of those 13 navies are U.S. allies or partners."

Is there any common sense or logic in this situation? Which way do you think a senator or a representative will vote if he or she represents a state in which businesses are awarded defense contracts? Keep in mind that the members of Congress also work to defend and support their emotional fingerprints. They might very well validate their emotional fingerprints by voting to increase the defense budget—and that, too, will be consistent with their belief systems.

When it comes to our emotional compasses, we don't all have the same "north star." We are not all aligned to the same focal point. What my belief system won't allow me to do, yours may require you to do. What seems illogical and incorrect to me may seem self-evident and obvious to you. Even if we share the same emotional fingerprint, our emotional compasses may send us off in vastly different directions to fulfill ourselves. My aspect of importance for being a good parent requires me to cut back on my working hours to spend time with my kids, to hug and kiss them, to play with them and do projects with them, and to try to be flexible and sensitive in disciplining them. Someone equally committed to the same aspect might believe that he has to work extra hours to support his family; to model for his children a serious, reserved, and stern demeanor to instill respect for authority; and to try to be strict and consistent when enforcing discipline. We both have an identical aspect of importance, but we have two hugely different emotional compasses, and each points to a completely different "true north."

I might not agree with Voliva, with our national defense policy, or with the hypothetical strict father, nor should you agree with beliefs or actions that you perceive as inaccurate or inappropriate. All of us need to take into account that other people have very different emotional compasses from ours and that they may not be interested in or even capable of behaving any differently. Being aware of their emotional compasses gives us a better chance of reaching them, whether to exchange opinions, arrange for compromise, or even change their minds. If there is no chance of altering their opinions, our awareness of their alternate views might mean that we can work out our differences.

Meanwhile, being aware of your own emotional compass can help you to make your own decisions, and becoming aware of your emotional fingerprint can give you the power to live consciously and to master your emotional highs and lows.

Now that we're fully aware of the emotional fingerprint (and how it is modified by the emotional compass), it's time to learn to internalize it.

PART II

Internalize Your Emotional Fingerprint

4

Discover Your Emotional Reserves

Man is free at the moment he wishes to be.
—Voltaire

One evening a wise Cherokee man sat by the fire and shared an old legend with his grandson. He described a battle that rages inside us all as a contest between two wolves. The first wolf represented anger, envy, jealousy, sorrow, regret, greed, arrogance, self-pity, guilt, resentment, inferiority, lies, false pride, superiority, and ego. The second wolf stood for joy, peace, love, hope, serenity, humility, kindness, benevolence, empathy, generosity, truth, compassion, and faith.

"These two wolves live in each of us," the grandfather explained. "They are constantly fighting. They are engaged in a battle for our souls."

The grandson thought for a minute, then asked, "Which one wins?"

The old man smiled at his grandson. "What you starve dies," he told the boy, "and what you feed grows. The wolf that wins is the one you feed."

We can see this battle in ourselves, our stories, and our culture. Just look at the message conveyed by the Declaration of Independence: "We hold these truths to be self-evident, that all men are created equal, that they are endowed by their Creator with certain unalienable Rights; that among these are Life, Liberty, and the pursuit of Happiness." Contrast those sentiments with the principles behind organizations like the Ku Klux Klan, which exist purely to spread the message of hatred based on race, religion, or sex. Do we feed our love of equality or our need to believe in racial, religious, or sexual superiority?

In popular culture we see this same concept metaphorically: as the Imperial forces versus the Jedi Knights in *Star Wars*, as Lord Voldemort versus Harry Potter in the Harry Potter series, or as the Volturi versus the Cullens in the Twilight Saga. In every story, the characters must choose: Will they serve the forces of freedom and love, or will they fan the flames of oppression and hate?

We are fascinated by this battle because we recognize this struggle between two forces so well. One is uplifting, hopeful, encouraging, confident, charitable, strong, free, and independent, seeking not to own or control. The other is fearful, egotistical, proud, arrogant, lazy, contentious, lonely, seeking both to control others and to win their approval.

We can see this fight in many movie plots and novels, but we can also see it in each of us. Some call it the battle between good and evil, but I prefer to call it the contest between internally and externally validating your emotional fingerprint.

What Does Internalizing Your Emotional Fingerprint Mean?

To help you grasp the difference between internally and externally validating your emotional fingerprint, let me tell you about my client Rita.

Rita was in her late forties. She had been married for twenty-five years to her college sweetheart and had always been faithful. She and her husband had two children, and they also ran a restaurant together. This was a business that the two of them had started with money they borrowed from Rita's family, and Rita vividly remembered the early days, when they had so little ready cash that they had to empty the change out of the vending machine in the restaurant lobby if they wanted to see a movie. Together they had worked hard and struggled for every penny. Finally, their kids went away to college, their business was successful, and they were financially comfortable and secure.

Then Rita's world fell apart. Her husband announced that with the children finally out of the house, he wanted a divorce. He told her that he had been having an affair for the past seven years, that he had lost interest in Rita sexually and romantically before that, and that he had been hanging on only for the sake of the children.

Rita was devastated. Although her husband was willing to make a financial settlement that would help her to make the transition into a new life, he made it clear that he would fight to keep the business. The divorce settlement they ultimately worked out allowed Rita a large lump sum, but eventually she would have to find another source of income. The children had mixed loyalties: Rita's daughter sided with her mother, but the son had always been closer to his dad and therefore sided with him. In one fell swoop, Rita felt the loss of her marriage, her employment, her financial future, and one of her children.

Here is the question I put to Rita: Do you consider yourself a failure or a success?

Initially, Rita was tempted to answer with a loud, resounding "Failure!" In fact, she had come to me describing her life with that very word. She had applied to work as a manager at some local restaurants, but because they had bitter memories of competing with Rita's former establishment, they weren't interested in hiring her now. She had gone back to school to become licensed as a respiratory therapist, but she had gotten Fs in her science courses because, she told me, "that stuff doesn't stick to my brain." She certainly considered her marriage to be a failure. She even had some regrets about how she had raised her children, since she saw in her son some of the same ruthless ambition she now recognized in her husband.

When Rita looked at her emotional fingerprint, she saw that her painful experience with her husband had disrespected every single aspect of importance: feeling confident in her appearance, being in a loving relationship, working, feeling secure, feeling validated, being a good parent, and feeling accepted.

"How can I validate my emotional fingerprint?" she asked me after she understood the concept. "No one finds me attractive, I'm *not* in a loving relationship, I'm not working, I've lost anything that ever made me feel secure, I'm being the opposite of validated or accepted, and with the kids out of the house, I don't really have the chance to be a good parent, especially with my son, who looks down on me the way his father does. What good does it do to know what makes me feel important when everything that *could* make me feel important is gone?"

Rita's self-evaluation was based on trying to have external factors validate her emotional fingerprint. It's true that Rita had not succeeded, if you looked at the external signs: what had happened to her marriage, her children, her job search, and her efforts at school. Judging from this perspective, it is easy to understand why Rita felt like a failure.

What would happen, however, if Rita validated her emotional fingerprint internally, defining her life not by external results but by her internal responses? Speaking internally, Rita could say that she behaved with integrity, strength, and compassion throughout her marriage, her child rearing, and her divorce. She had certainly made some mistakes, and she had some regrets, but she could also see much to be proud of in her conduct and many reasons to validate and accept herself.

Likewise, she could look at the creativity, dedication, and hard work she had put into the restaurant that she and her husband had owned. Although the restaurant was no longer hers, the qualities she had used to create it still were. Perhaps her latest efforts had not worked out well, but Rita could be proud of the qualities she brought to them—the same creativity, dedication, and hard work that she had relied on all her life.

Here's how Rita might have validated the seven disrespected aspects of her emotional fingerprint, if she had truly internalized them:

- Feeling confident in my appearance. I will focus every day on eating in a healthy way, getting enough sleep, and exercising at least thirty minutes a day. If on some days I don't achieve these goals, I will forgive myself and try again the next day.

- Being in a loving relationship. I was loving and caring in my marriage, even though things didn't work out. I continue to be the same loving, generous person I was when my husband and I were together. When I am ready to be in a relationship again, I will still be that person.

- Working. I did a good job founding and comanaging the restaurant, and I know that whatever job I get in the future will be lucky to have me, because I will be a person of dedication and integrity. I will work hard at researching my options and pursuing them effectively.

- Feeling secure. I can't control what my husband and my children do, but I know I can rely on myself. I will forgive my husband, which will help me to achieve emotional security, since by forgiving him I take away his power to hurt me, upset me, or throw me off balance. I will do everything in my power to make good choices and to prepare myself for my next career, to create the financial security I want.

- Feeling validated. I validate my past and what I have overcome. I validate my purpose on earth. I will keep a list of all of the positive things I do each day. By validating myself, I will free myself from the need to have others validate me.

- Being a good parent. I will accept my children for who they are, regardless of how they feel about me or what they are currently doing. That is the best gift a parent can give, and by giving them that acceptance now, I can make up for any shortcomings in my past.

- Feeling accepted. I accept myself for a loving, caring, and competent person who brought many good things to my marriage, my family, and my work experience. Because I accept myself, I am less concerned about whether others accept me.

When Rita externalized her emotional fingerprint, she had to consider herself a failure. When she internalized her emotional fingerprint—based not on the results of her actions but on the actions themselves—she could see herself as successful. More important, she could focus entirely on her own actions and responses in the future, letting go of the external results. She could ask herself each day not "Did I get a job?" or "Did I meet a new potential husband?" but rather "Did I behave in a way that I can be proud of?"

All of us are going to run into obstacles and setbacks at some time in our lives. Very few humans reach a ripe old age without having had at least some challenges in their personal lives, relationships, and careers. Politicians lose elections. Captains of industry go broke. Long-term marriages end in divorce. Children get involved with drugs, gambling, or bad companions. We all struggle with health, economic, relationship, and family problems. It's part of the human condition.

Nevertheless, we all have a choice about which wolf to feed: the one that asks us to look at external results or the one that encourages us to look within. If we define success externally, we have to accept that we are going to fail a good deal of the time, because external success is beyond our control. If we define success internally, as Rita eventually learned to do, we can potentially succeed 100 percent of the time. We can always choose to behave in a way that we are proud of, to give ourselves the validation and support that we desire, to focus on our actions and not on our outcomes. Viewed internally, success is always within our control. When we feed *that* wolf—the wolf of internalizing our emotional fingerprints—we develop tremendous emotional reserves.

Internalizing Your Emotional Fingerprint

Evaluate one part of your life: personal life, relationships, or business. Identify how you are validating each aspect of your emotional fingerprint, both internally and externally.

Use the following example of Rosemary Lyons, a public relations specialist and the single mother of two teenagers, who chose to focus on relationships:

My Emotional Fingerprint	External	Internal
1. In control	I'm not in control of my teenagers, who seem to be getting into a lot of trouble lately.	I control my temper with my kids.
2. Given respect	My teens don't seem to respect my efforts to discipline them.	I respect myself for being a patient mom.
3. Praise	My kids don't praise me for all the hard work I do for them.	I can praise myself for doing the best I can right now as a mom.
4. Being creative	I haven't worked on anything really creative in a long time.	I have found creative ways to solve my problems on my own.
5. Solving problems	I don't think I have solved many problems lately!	My definition of a good problem solver is one who never gives up.
6. Being a good parent	My kids are not happy, and I am not solving their problems for them.	My definition of being a good mom is never giving up on my kids and always loving them.
7. Winning	Everything I do is turning out badly, so I must be losing.	A winner, in my book, is someone who follows her conscience and is good to the people she loves.

Chose one area of your life to focus on—personal life, relationships, or business—and complete the exercise for that area:

My Emotional Fingerprint	External	Internal
1. _____	_____	_____
	_____	_____
	_____	_____
2. _____	_____	_____
	_____	_____
	_____	_____
3. _____	_____	_____
	_____	_____
	_____	_____
4. _____	_____	_____
	_____	_____
	_____	_____
5. _____	_____	_____
	_____	_____
	_____	_____
6. _____	_____	_____
	_____	_____
	_____	_____
7. _____	_____	_____
	_____	_____
	_____	_____

What Are Emotional Reserves?

Emotional reserves are an inner source of strength, the ability one has to withstand a challenge, a setback, or an obstacle. Have you ever wondered how some people manage to overcome extraordinarily difficult circumstances, withstand enormous challenges, and keep trying again and again, even after a number of apparent failures? These people have unusually well-developed emotional reserves that support their resilience, their persistence, and their optimism. Their emotional reserves enable them to keep going when others in their place might well give up. Their emotional reserves also permit them to behave with generosity, compassion, or joy when others in their place might act rudely, selfishly, or despairingly. When you reach deep down in yourself and find the last little bit of extra strength—and then a bit more, and then a bit more—you are drawing on your emotional reserves.

We fill our emotional reserves through validation of the emotional fingerprint. As we saw in chapter 2, validating at least two aspects of one's emotional fingerprint creates an emotional high. It also is a kind of deposit into our storehouse of emotional reserves. When we feel important—which we achieve by validating at least one aspect of our emotional fingerprints—we become stronger, clearer, more energized, and happier. The more often we feel important and the more deeply we feel important, the more our emotional reserves grow. Then when we face life's challenges, we can draw on those reserves. They are there to replenish us whenever we feel low.

One of the most inspiring stories I know of emotional reserves is that of the philosopher Viktor Frankl. Frankl lost every member of his family in the Holocaust and, as a concentration camp inmate, endured some of the bitterest circumstances that humans have ever experienced. Yet he emerged from the horror with a renewed faith in the power of love and in humans' ability to choose a path for themselves, no matter what was done to them.

"We who lived in concentration camps can remember the men who walked through the huts comforting others, giving away their last piece of bread," Frankl wrote in his extraordinary book *Man's Search for Meaning*. "They may have been few in number, but they offer sufficient proof that everything can be taken from a man but one thing: the last of the human freedoms—to choose one's attitude in any given set of circumstances, to choose one's own way."

To validate one's emotional fingerprint internally is to choose one's own way, and as Frankl's example shows, making that choice creates tremendous emotional reserves. Internalizing one's emotional fingerprint also means enjoying life more intensely—again, even under horrific circumstances. Look at how Frankl describes the prisoners' relationship to nature:

> As the inner life of the prisoner tended to become more intense, he also experienced the beauty of art and nature as never before. Under their influence he sometimes even forgot his own frightful circumstances. If someone had seen our faces on the journey from Auschwitz to a Bavarian camp as we beheld the mountains of Salzburg with their summits glowing in the sunset, through the little barred windows of the prison carriage, he would never have believed that those were the faces of men who had given up all hope of life and liberty. Despite that factor—or maybe because of it—we were carried away by nature's beauty, which we had missed for so long.
>
> In camp too, a man might draw the attention of a comrade working next to him to a nice view of the setting sun shining through the tall trees of the Bavarian woods . . . the same woods in which we had built an enormous, hidden munitions plant. One evening, when we were already resting on the floor of our hut, dead tired, soup bowls in hand, a fellow prisoner rushed in and asked us to run out to the assembly grounds and see the wonderful sunset. Standing outside we saw sinister clouds glowing in the west and the whole sky alive with clouds of ever-changing shapes and colors, from steel blue to blood red. The desolate grey mud huts provided a sharp contrast, while the puddles on the muddy ground reflected the glowing sky. Then, after minutes of moving silence, one prisoner said to another, "How beautiful the world could be!"

Think for a moment about what Frankl is telling us. Here is a group of prisoners who are freezing, starving, and exhausted. They know that all of their loved ones are suffering, too, or perhaps their families are already dead. They have no real possibility of escape and very little hope of being set free. They are completely at the mercy of brutal guards and have every expectation of being beaten, tortured, or killed. Yet they manage to find the emotional reserves to marvel at a sunset. If they can find moments of joy and wonder in the midst of their lives, why can't the rest of us do the same?

Another inspiring example of internalizing the emotional fingerprint is Nelson Mandela, the South African freedom fighter (and future president) who was imprisoned on Robben Island for twenty-seven years. Mandela too must often have thought that his life would end in prison, with little chance of seeing the end of racial apartheid in his homeland. He must have wondered whether his life, his struggles, and his suffering had all come to nothing, whether there was any meaning in the sacrifices he had made. Separated from his wife and his children, at the mercy of guards who hated and feared him, he might easily have grown bitter and despairing or perhaps vengeful and angry.

Instead, by all accounts, he spent his time in prison rousing his fellow prisoners to fight for their rights and encouraging them to feel hopeful about the future. When he emerged from prison, he set a course of reconciliation and forgiveness for his country. As inspiringly chronicled in the movie *Invictus*, he invited even the former supporters of the apartheid regime to help build the new South Africa.

The movie takes its name from a poem by William Ernest Henley that Mandela found inspiring; its message helped him to survive the brutal experience of prison on his own terms. I find it inspiring, too, so I'm going to share part of it with you here:

> Out of the night that covers me,
> Black as the Pit from pole to pole,
> I thank whatever gods may be
> For my unconquerable soul.
> In the fell clutch of circumstance
> I have not winced nor cried aloud.
> Under the bludgeoning of chance
> My head is bloody, but unbowed.
>
> . . .

It matters not how strait the gate,
How charged with punishments the scroll.
I am the master of my fate:
I am the captain of my soul.

For Mandela, in prison with no hope of release, these words of Henley reminded him that *he*, not his jailers, was the master of his fate and the captain of his soul. This is the very essence of internalizing your emotional fingerprint. Its reward can be vividly seen in Mandela's extraordinary emotional reserves.

These two examples of imprisoned men may seem like extreme examples, but are they, really? Do you know people who have mentally or emotionally imprisoned themselves? Do you know anyone who is crippled by fear or rejection? What about someone who has been hurt in a relationship and now seems incapable of connecting romantically with others? We do not have to live through impoverished conditions to apply the techniques that saved these men's lives. From the research and interviews I

Running on Empty

Have you ever

- Yelled at your romantic partner or your kids for no reason?
- Snipped at your best friend for something that was not his or her fault?
- Felt like the whole world was going to come crashing down on you if your boss assigned you one more deadline?
- Let an angry sales clerk or an unresponsive customer-service representative ruin your day?

When you blow up for no apparent reason or let little things get to you, you know that your emotional reserves are getting low. Replenish them by validating at least two aspects of your emotional fingerprint, and you'll find yourself feeling better right away.

have conducted, I can assure you that mental prisons can be just as confining and restrictive as physical ones. You must create emotional reserves to tear down the walls of confinement.

Ordinary Circumstances, Extraordinary Lives

I've chosen some extraordinary examples to introduce the concept of emotional reserves because I want you to see just how far your own emotional reserves can take you, but internalizing your emotional fingerprint can work just as well in more ordinary circumstances. In fact, as I've seen time and again in my own life, my marriage, and the lives of my clients, internalizing the emotional fingerprint can transform an ordinary life into an extraordinary life.

I have two sons: Hunter, who is ten, and Pierce, who is seven. Although I dearly love both my children, I know that every day presents many opportunities for power struggles: little fights, like getting them out of bed in the morning, or the huge screaming tantrums that can take place when one (or all) of us is really tired.

What helps me to avoid those power struggles and gives me the emotional reserves to deal with the stresses and strains of parenting is my ability to internalize my emotional fingerprint, along with my awareness of my kids' emotional fingerprints. Hunter, for example, has a strong aspect of importance of being in control. I used to come into his bedroom each morning and remind him that he had to get up, make his bed, and put his clothes in the laundry. This was the recipe for an instant fight, but I couldn't stand the thought of him leaving his room a shambles, and I didn't want either me or my wife to have to keep cleaning up after him.

Then I began to work *with* Hunter's need to be in control instead of butting heads with him over it. I realized that if I gave him something to control, his emotional fingerprint would be validated, and I could still get what I wanted from him. Now when I come into his room to ask him to clean up, I say, "Hunter, here's all the stuff that needs to get done today—*when* do you want to do it?" Knowing that he's in control makes all the difference: he gets his chores done, I let go of my need to have him do what I say when I say it, and both of us are free to enjoy each other rather than fight.

Hunter's younger brother, Pierce, just wants to play. One aspect of his emotional fingerprint is, like mine, being free and independent, and he expresses his freedom through play. Pierce also has the aspect of importance of experiencing life, so he just throws himself into his activities. That kid can outplay anybody!

If I remember how important play is to Pierce—how important it makes him feel—I can overcome my own tendency to just chill out at the end of the day rather than playing intensely with my son. I can treasure the fact that he still wants me to "help him play" rather than choosing to focus on his friends or on activities that don't include me. I can also work out a compromise with him: I'll play with him for fifteen minutes at anything he chooses if he is then willing to give me some space to recuperate from my own long, intense day.

Hunter and Pierce both love to make things out of Legos, which they tend to scatter across our living room floor as they become absorbed in construction. I hate clutter, so my first impulse on seeing the messy floor is to yell at my sons. "I worked all day long, so get those toys off the floor—I'm sick of stepping on Legos!"

Instead, I try to remind myself of my sons' emotional fingerprints and of what it was like for me when I was a kid. I recall how frustrated I was that none of the grown-ups seemed to understand how much I loved playing, how restricted I always felt by having to follow their ideas of what I should do instead of following my own ideas. So when I see my sons' creative efforts spread all over our floor, I say, "Boys, I love what you're working on, but I don't want to keep tripping over it. What do *you* think we should do?" It doesn't always work, but it often does. Instead of a fight, we have the chance to make a game out of the cleanup process. Instead of being an ordinary parent, I have the opportunity to foster an extraordinary relationship with my sons.

What about your life? Do you have the chance to turn your ordinary marriage into an extraordinary relationship that nourishes, challenges, and supports both you and your spouse in ever-deepening ways? Can you see the possibility of becoming an extraordinary employee or entrepreneur who always goes the extra mile or volunteers for the job no one else wants? Can you perhaps be the one who raises his or her hand and says "Stop!" when no one else has the courage to identify a problem? Does becoming extraordinary interest you as a way of getting more value and pleasure out of your life?

The wonderful thing about internalizing your emotional fingerprint is that it gives you far greater emotional reserves. Since your own needs are already met, you have the clarity to think of the needs of others, so you become more caring and supportive, as I have tried to be with my sons. You also have a greater ability to take advantage of business opportunities or to respond more flexibly to economic challenges; when you see new possibilities, you have the reserves to take them on.

Discovering your emotional reserves isn't about doing more, exactly; rather, it's about doing more with less. If you've got only ten minutes to play with your kids, you can see how to make that ten minutes really count, because it's based on each child's emotional fingerprint and not your own. If you're facing monster deadlines and you have only a few minutes to talk to your wife at the end of the day, you can really be emotionally present with her so that she then has the resources to make it through the times you're busy and stressed. If you can't give your friends or your relatives the amount of time they deserve, you can at least find ways to let them know that you love them and you're there. Because your emotional reserves are already full, you have plenty to share, even if you can't do everything you might like. Replenishing your emotional reserves by giving your "internal wolf" the nourishment it needs means, in the end, that everybody in your life benefits.

EXERCISE

Exploring Your Emotional Reserves

Evaluate your emotional reserves in each domain of your life by answering the following questions. Use the example of Jared Craig, a forty-five-year-old information technology middle manager:

Personal Life

1. Circle the choice that best completes the following sentence: In my personal life, my emotional reserves are:

   High   Medium   (Low)

2. Something in my personal life that disrespects my emotional fingerprint and drains my emotional reserves is: My mother is elderly, and because my sister lives in another city, I have the primary responsibility for taking care of Mom. She often expects me to drop everything at a moment's notice if she needs something, and if I don't, she tells my sister, who calls or e-mails me to ask why I'm not more helpful.

   The aspects of importance that this situation disrespects: being trusted, being free and independent.

3. Something in my personal life that validates my emotional fingerprint and replenishes my emotional reserves is: My friend Ben and I play racquetball together every Thursday and then go out for a drink and maybe dinner. We mainly talk sports, but sometimes other subjects come up. He's a good friend, and we can count on each other.

   The aspects of importance that this situation validates: being trusted, being in the moment.

4. Three things I could do to replenish my emotional reserves by validating my emotional fingerprint in my personal life are:

Aspect	Validation
Trusted	I could live my life worthy of trust so I know I can count on myself to keep my promises to others and myself.
Connected to family	I could focus more on my own idea of being a good son so I wouldn't feel guilty when my mother and my sister start in—I would know I could count on myself to do the right thing.
Connected to nature	I could see about getting out in the country every other Sunday for a hike or a walk in the woods.

Now it's your turn.

Personal Life

1. Circle the choice that best completes the following sentence: In my personal life, my emotional reserves are:

   High   Medium   Low

2. Something in my personal life that disrespects my emotional fingerprint and drains my emotional reserves is:

   _____

   _____

   The aspects of importance that this situation disrespects are:

   _____

   _____

3. Something in my personal life that validates my emotional fingerprint and replenishes my emotional reserves is:

   _____

   _____

   The aspects of importance that this situation validates are:

   _____

   _____

4. Three things I could do to replenish my emotional reserves by validating my emotional fingerprint in my personal life are:

   Aspect   Validation

   _____   _____

   _____   _____

   _____   _____

Relationships

1. Circle the choice that best completes the following sentence: In my relationships, my emotional reserves are:

   High   Medium   Low

2. Something in my relationships that disrespects my emotional fingerprint and drains my emotional reserves is:

   _____

   _____

The aspects of importance that this situation disrespects are:

_____

_____

3. Something in my relationships that validates my emotional finger-print and replenishes my emotional reserves is:

_____

_____

The aspects of importance that this situation validates are:

_____

_____

4. Three things I could do to replenish my emotional reserves by validating my emotional fingerprint in my relationships are:

Aspect   Validation

_____   _____

_____   _____

_____   _____

Career or Work Life

1. Circle the choice that best completes the following sentence: In my career or work life, my emotional reserves are:
   High   Medium   Low

2. Something in my career or work life that disrespects my emotional fingerprint and drains my emotional reserves is:

_____

_____

The aspects of importance that this situation disrespects are:

_____

_____

3. Something in my career or work life that validates my emotional fingerprint and replenishes my emotional reserves is:

_____

_____

The aspects of importance that this situation validates are:

_____

_____

4. Three things I could do to replenish my emotional reserves by validating my emotional fingerprint in my career or work life are:

Aspect   Validation

_____   _____

_____   _____

_____   _____

Filling Up the Tank

In chapter 6, you'll learn ways to expand your emotional reserves that are specific to your emotional fingerprint. Now we will learn the ten universal ways to expand your reserves; these work for everybody, because they help you to shift from external to internal validation and then keep you practicing that approach. The ten universal ways to expand your emotional reserves are as follows:

1. *Live in gratitude.* The fastest way to stop feeding the external wolf and start feeding the internal one is to make a list of things you are grateful for. I tell my clients to list fifty things every day for a week—and they can never list the same thing twice. By the third day, most people are expressing gratitude for tube socks and pillowcases, but it helps to remind you that someone out there would kill for your problems, because your problems seem so incomparably better than their problems.

2. *Forgive.* One of the worst injuries we can do to ourselves is to hold on to anger, grudges, resentment, and betrayal by refusing to forgive others. Even worse, though, is when we fail to forgive ourselves. If you're feeling drained and depleted, find a reason to forgive yourself or someone else.

3. *Give yourself the gift of time*. Even fifteen minutes of doing whatever you want and having no obligations can have a healing effect and leave you feeling refreshed and restored.

4. *Pamper yourself*. Treating yourself like someone who is valuable helps you to view life from the inside out rather than the outside in.

5. *Play*. Take a page from my son Pierce's book and find something to play at that releases your inner depths of enthusiasm and joy. A sport, a game, a puzzle, a set of cartwheels—anything that lets you throw yourself into the activity with complete abandon will do the trick.

6. *Read something*. Just taking some time from your day to read and think can help you to reconnect with your own wisdom.

7. *Meditate and pray*. Listening to the still, small voice within is a terrific way to internalize your emotional fingerprint.

8. *Engage in creative activities*. Make a special card for someone you love. Write a poem. Take a dance class. Join a chorus. Help your kids to make an elaborate gingerbread house or a popsicle-stick castle. Doing something creative can remind you that you can also re-create yourself.

9. *Do some selfless service*. Going beyond yourself is, paradoxically, one of the best ways to get in touch with yourself. Rediscover your compassion—and your passion.

10. *Find some new hobbies*. I'm a big believer in learning something new periodically throughout your life. Having to grow and stretch, even in little ways, reminds you that you can always count on yourself to have the resources you need.

Which Wolf Do You Feed?

The amazing thing about learning to internalize your emotional fingerprint is that you immediately feel such positive emotional effects. When you externalize your emotional fingerprint—that is, when you look to external results for your validation—you cannot help but feel a whole slew of negative emotions.

For example, when my client Rita looked at external results— her broken marriage, her troubled children, her lost business—she felt despairing, lonely, sad, frustrated, and incomplete. She envied her friends who were still married. She envied her single friends who were successfully dating or who seemed happier being single. She compared herself to parents whose kids were having an easier time, and she felt disappointed in herself and her children. She thought of the husband who had betrayed her with another woman and felt resentful, jealous, and sometimes even filled with hate. She looked at everything she was going to have to do to rebuild her life and felt overloaded, exhausted, and fearful. She experienced her life as one of scarcity, and she experienced the world around her as hostile.

As we worked together, Rita learned to internalize her emotional fingerprint. She found ways to validate her aspects of importance and define her life in internal rather than external terms. The shift in her emotional outlook was remarkable.

Instead of looking at external results, Rita began to look at who she was: a courageous survivor who loved her kids and who had still not given up on love even though she had had a terrible experience. She found ways to validate the six disrespected aspects of her emotional fingerprint: feeling confident in her appearance, being in a loving relationship, working, feeling secure, feeling validated, and being a good parent.

Rita started biking on the weekends and reconnected to her body in a new way, which gave her a new sense of confidence in her appearance that was not dependent on anyone's judgment of her but that grew from the inside. Although she wasn't ready to date yet, she wrote in her journal about what she thought a good relationship should be and focused on developing the qualities that she thought would make her a better partner in a future relationship: generosity, assertiveness, and a strong, clear judgment that could not be swayed by others' responses. Instead of feeling despair, she felt hope. Instead of being frustrated, she felt a sense of accomplishment. Instead of feeling incomplete, she began to feel whole. Instead of feeling only sorrow, she often experienced periods of joy, as though she were coming to the surface again after a long, long time underwater.

Internalizing her emotional fingerprint also meant that Rita was no longer lonely all the time. Although she had to let go of some old friends who were threatened by her single status or who didn't appreciate the kind of emotional work she was doing, she felt closer than ever to her remaining friends, and those relationships became deeper than they had ever been. Instead of feeling envy, Rita felt pleasure in her friends' achievements, because she herself was experiencing the fullness of her own emotional reserves.

She was able to forgive her husband—not to agree with his actions or to excuse what he did, but to let go of her anger, resentment, and jealousy so that she genuinely didn't care anymore what he did. Instead of feeling overloaded and exhausted, she felt energized and enthusiastic. Instead of being fearful, she felt brave. She no longer experienced her life as one of scarcity but instead experienced the world as a welcoming, abundant place from which she could get what she wanted out of life.

As Rita internalized her emotional fingerprint, her emotional reserves continued to deepen. She began to notice other changes in her life as a result. Her children became more open to her and more interested in spending time with her. Rita began to realize how needy and insecure she had been before and how her unsatisfying life with her husband had caused her to turn to her kids for emotional support. In response, they had shied away. Now that Rita didn't need as much from them, they became more interested in being with her and in offering freely the emotional support that she had tried to force from them before.

"I still have a lot of questions about my life, and there are a lot of things I still want to work on," Rita told me at our last session. "But I feel like now I'm looking to myself for the answers and not to anyone else. Being aware of my emotional fingerprint means that I know who I am and what makes me feel important.

Internalizing my emotional fingerprint means that I can make *myself* feel important, anytime I want to, simply by validating my aspects of importance. It's an amazing feeling."

I was happy to agree.

When you compare the results of externalizing your emotional fingerprint with what happens when you internalize it, you can see clearly the benefits of being internal. Take a look at the different outcomes that come from these two different approaches:

Externalizing Your Emotional Fingerprint

Anger	Loss
Envy	Ego
Sorrow	Disappointment
Jealousy	Sense of being overloaded
Fear	Frustration
Fatigue	Covetousness
Sense of being overwhelmed	Gossip
Sadness	Feeling of incompletion
Exhaustion	Hatred
Pride	Scarcity
Loneliness	

Internalizing Your Emotional Fingerprint

Peace	Leadership
Happiness	Productivity
Confidence	Charity
Strength	Endurance
Energy	Hope
Love	Longevity
Kindness	Abundance
Gratitude	Patience
Humility	Forgiveness
Power	Control

Moving from Externalizing to Internalizing

Evaluate your emotional reserves in each domain of your life by answering the following questions. Use the example of Roberta Lazar, who has an entry-level job at a small magazine:

1. Identify a situation in your work life or career in which you were looking for external validation. It could be a situation in the present, or it might be a vivid memory from the past.

   Situation in which I externalize my emotional fingerprint: At my job, you can either be doing office work or they can assign you to a story. I worry a lot about whether I am getting as many assignments as the other kids who work there. Sometimes it seems like I'm doing an awful lot of office work!

   What results do I get when I externalize my emotional fingerprint in that situation? Envy, anxiety, resentment, sadness, disappointment, frustration, backbiting, gossip, scarcity.

   What are two ways I could internalize my emotional fingerprint in that situation by internally validating two or more aspects of my emotional fingerprint?

   • Aspect of my emotional fingerprint: Being in control

     How I could validate it: I can accept the fact that I can't control how many assignments I get (even if I can maybe affect my situation by working hard and doing a good job—not the same as being in control!). But if I'm really internalizing my emotional fingerprint, maybe I'm not thinking about how to get them to assign me stories at all. Maybe instead I should focus on being a good reporter: coming up with great story ideas, working hard on every story I write, maybe finding a way to publish something on a blog or a community paper where they will be happy to have me. Then I would be doing work that I love, and I'd feel in control of that.

   • Aspect of my emotional fingerprint: Learning

     How I could validate it: I could try to learn all I can about the magazine and about publishing and journalism in general. I can't control the assignments I get, but nobody can stop me from learning! (Learning more will make me a better reporter, and then I'll feel more in control of reporting well, even if I'm not getting good assignments very often.)

Now it's your turn.

1. Identify a situation in your work life or career in which you were looking for external validation. It could be a situation in the present, or it might be a vivid memory from the past.

    Situation in which I externalize my emotional fingerprint:

    _____

    _____

    What results do I get when I externalize my emotional fingerprint in that situation?

    _____

    _____

    What are two ways I could internalize my emotional fingerprint in that situation by internally validating two or more aspects of my emotional fingerprint?

    Aspect of my emotional fingerprint:

    _____

    How I could validate it:

    _____

    _____

    Aspect of my emotional fingerprint:

    _____

    How I could validate it:

    _____

    _____

2. Identify a situation in your relationships in which you were looking for external validation. It could be a situation in the present, or it might be a vivid memory from the past.

    Situation in which I externalize my emotional fingerprint:

    _____

    _____

What results do I get when I externalize my emotional fingerprint in that situation?

_____

_____

What are two ways I could internalize my emotional fingerprint in that situation by internally validating two or more aspects of my emotional fingerprint?

Aspect of my emotional fingerprint:

_____

How I could validate it:

_____

_____

Aspect of my emotional fingerprint:

_____

How I could validate it:

_____

_____

3. Identify a situation in your personal life in which you were looking for external validation. It could be a situation in the present, or it might be a vivid memory from the past.

Situation in which I externalize my emotional fingerprint:

_____

_____

What results do I get when I externalize my emotional fingerprint in that situation?

_____

_____

What are two ways I could internalize my emotional fingerprint in that situation by internally validating two or more aspects of my emotional fingerprint?

Aspect of my emotional fingerprint:

_____

How I could validate it:

_____

_____

Aspect of my emotional fingerprint:

_____

How I could validate it:

_____

_____

_____

Acceptance versus Resignation

You're probably familiar with the Serenity Prayer: "Lord, grant me the courage to change the things I can, the serenity to accept the things I can't, and the wisdom to know the difference." That wisdom is part of internalizing your emotional fingerprint, for I am certainly not counseling you to blindly accept any restriction or obstacle you encounter—just the opposite. Some of the heroes I cited earlier in this book, like Viktor Frankl, Nelson Mandela, and Harriet Tubman, took extraordinary risks to resist, fight back, and encourage others to join them in changing or escaping oppressive situations.

Paradoxically, though, what gave them the strength to change the external world was their extraordinary emotional reserves, which came from internalizing their emotional fingerprints and seeking validation for them from within. I urge you to start following in their footsteps by feeding your internal wolf and letting the external one starve. I promise you that you'll be very glad you did.

5

Protect Your Emotional Fingerprint

> We tend to forget that happiness doesn't come as a
> result of getting something we don't have, but rather
> of recognizing and appreciating what we do have.
> —Frederick Keonig

My client Jenna was frustrated. She had become aware of her emotional fingerprint, which helped her to understand what made her happy and what she really wanted in life. She had begun to internalize her emotional fingerprint and was just starting to tap into some unsuspected emotional reserves. Nevertheless, she was still not satisfied with many aspects of her life, and she didn't understand why.

Jenna was a devoted teacher of computer skills at a local specialty public high school. She would seemingly stop at nothing to help her students, many of whom were from troubled inner-city neighborhoods. To motivate and inspire her students, Jenna started a school website. She arranged for the university basketball team to donate tickets, so that any students who fulfilled the class requirements could attend a game as a reward. She spent hours tutoring individual students who needed help, meeting with parents who didn't understand the value of what she was doing, and visiting local businesses to solicit donations for the school's computer lab. Her dedication was extraordinary, and I admired her for it.

Jenna was also a gifted artist who spent so much time serving her students that she didn't have time for her own painting. When we identified the aspects of importance of her emotional fingerprint, we realized that two of them were in conflict: being creative and serving.

"I feel important when I'm being creative—*and* when I'm serving," Jenna eventually told me. "I feel frustrated when I'm not giving my all to my students, because I see how much they need and how much my work can benefit them. But I haven't painted in months, and I really miss it. I can't just pick up a brush for ten or fifteen minutes at the end of the day—I'm too tired from teaching, and I need big chunks of time to really be creative. And I can't do a halfhearted job at school—not when I look at my students' faces! So what do I do here? How do I validate both of those aspects of my emotional fingerprint?"

When Aspects of Your Emotional Fingerprint Conflict

Jenna's conflict moved me, because it went right to the heart of what mattered most to her in life. She had identified what made her feel important—being creative and serving—and had found two activities that allowed her to validate both of these aspects. She had also begun to internalize these aspects of her emotional fingerprint. She wasn't looking for admiration or expecting anyone else to validate her efforts. All she wanted was a chance to do her work, whether teaching or painting. She was doing everything right, yet she had stumbled on a seemingly irresolvable conflict.

Many of my clients—and many people I know—run into similar conflicts. Following are some of the most common. Can you think of others?

Conflict	Possible Conflicting Aspects of Emotional Fingerprint
Wanting to rise high in a profession	Providing, overcoming challenges, working, receiving recognition, achieving my life's purpose, reaching my goals, winning
versus	versus
Wanting to be a good parent	Being connected to family, being a good parent
Wanting to care for an elderly parent	Being connected to family, honoring my standards
versus	versus
Fulfilling responsibilities to spouse and children	Being in a loving relationship, being a good parent
Needing to put in extra hours at work	Providing, overcoming challenges, working, receiving recognition, achieving my life's purpose, reaching my goals, winning
versus	versus
Needing time outside	Being connected to nature
Wanting to hang out with close friends	Being a friend
versus	versus
Spending time with a romantic partner or spouse	Being in a loving relationship
Wanting financial security for self and/or family	Providing, working, being secure, being a good parent, honoring my standards
versus	versus
Wanting to start a business, go back to school, change jobs, or begin a new profession	Being in control, being respected, being free and independent, being creative, receiving recognition, achieving my life's purpose, winning
Wanting to care for spouse and kids	Providing, being in a loving relationship, being connected to family, being a good parent, being needed, honoring my standards, serving

(continued)

Conflict versus Needing some time for self	Possible Conflicting Aspects of Emotional Fingerprint versus Being connected to God, spirit, or the universe; being free and independent; being creative; receiving recognition; being connected to nature; learning; experiencing life

Sometimes people experience conflicts *within* their emotional fingerprints:

- Possible conflicts within "being a good parent":

    Cushioning your children from life's blows versus helping them to become independent and self-reliant

    Giving your children everything they need versus teaching them about limits and doing without

    Encouraging your children to be brave and to take risks versus showing them how to be appropriately cautious

    Supporting your children's creativity and big dreams versus asking them to be realistic and sensible

- Possible conflicts within "being in a loving relationship":

    Supporting the other person versus taking time for yourself

    Sharing interests versus having your own interests

    Being honest versus being supportive

    Giving the other person a break when he or she is having a hard time versus protecting yourself and not being taken advantage of

- Possible conflicts within "experiencing life":

    Sampling many new places versus exploring one place in depth

    Trying out many different activities versus experiencing the joys of focusing and becoming an expert

    Seeking activities that require effort versus enjoying the pleasures of relaxing and letting life come to you

    Experiencing life on your own versus experiencing life with a partner

The lists could go on and on. When we are young, we might think that there is one right way to live, one magical approach that will solve all of our problems. As we get older, however, we realize that life is full of conflicts and that it isn't always possible to avoid them. The challenge is to handle our conflicts in productive, effective ways that leave us feeling satisfied with our choices. Sometimes we have a conflict between two wonderful alternatives, sometimes we're choosing between the lesser of two evils, and often we're choosing between two sets of compromises with pros and cons to each.

How can you handle conflict in a way that protects your emotional fingerprint?

E X E R C I S E

Identifying Your Conflicts

This is an exercise in identifying your conflicts. I've filled it in first with my own conflicts and how I deal with them so you can get some idea how to complete the exercise with your own concerns:

1. Identify three conflicts in your life.
   a. Spending too much time at work versus not enough time with my family
   b. Spending time being creative versus working
   c. Experiencing life versus juggling work and family responsibilities
2. Describe how each conflict is draining your emotional reserves.
   a. My wife and I have an amazing relationship, but sometimes book and movie deadlines interfere with family time and vacation time. My intention is to always put my family first, but sometimes my business screams for attention.
   b. If I were retired, I would paint and sculpt all day long. It wouldn't matter if I ever sold one painting, but to just have the time to be creative would be wonderful. With the demands of my business, it is challenging to find the time to be creative.

    c. I would love to backpack across Europe, sail the seven seas, and climb the highest mountains, but the cost of growing up has made that dream difficult.

3. Identify the aspects of importance of your emotional fingerprint that are involved in each conflict.

    a. Providing, being a good parent, being creative, achieving my life's purpose, experiencing life, and feeling connected to God, spirit, or the universe

    b. Being creative, providing, being free and independent versus being a good parent, and experiencing life

    c. Experiencing life, achieving my life's purpose, feeling free and independent versus providing, and being a good parent

Now identify your struggles and how you deal with them.

1. Identify three conflicts in your life.

    a. _____ versus _____

    b. _____ versus _____

    c. _____ versus _____

2. Describe how each conflict is draining your emotional reserves.

    a. _____

    b. _____

    c. _____

3. Identify the aspects of importance of your emotional fingerprint that are involved in each conflict.

    a. _____

    b. _____

    c. _____

What Happens When You Don't Protect Your Emotional Fingerprint

When you are faced with the kinds of internal conflicts we just examined, you might fail to protect your emotional fingerprint. As a result, your emotional reserves become depleted. You find it harder to validate your emotional fingerprint, you lose control of your emotional ups and downs, and you begin to dishonor your emotional compass, pushing yourself to act in ways that don't feel right to you.

You might try harder to please and placate those around you, or you might find yourself picking fights, getting into power struggles, or generally becoming annoyed and resentful. You feel frayed, frustrated, and burned out, easily overcome by little things, without the resilience or resourcefulness that you'd like. You might feel drained, exhausted, discouraged, depressed, angry, or simply confused as you withdraw emotionally and try to avoid the conflict rather than facing it head-on. Worst of all, you stop internalizing your emotional fingerprint and start externalizing it, looking to other people or circumstances to make you feel important rather than finding ways to make yourself feel that way.

Why do we fall into these responses? In my view, there are three primary reasons. Any of these could be a problem for you, together or separately:

- You ignore your emotional fingerprint by denying that your conflicts exist.
- You ignore your emotional fingerprint by dishonoring your limits.
- You externalize your emotional fingerprint by comparing yourself unfavorably to others and seeking external validation in other ways.

Let's take a closer look.

Ignoring Your Emotional Fingerprint: Denying That Your Conflicts Exist

When I first helped Jenna identify her emotional fingerprint, I was immediately struck by her aspect of importance of being creative. I asked her where in her life that aspect was being validated, and for a moment she looked confused.

"I think I'm creative in coming up with projects for my students," she finally said, and I agreed that she certainly was. Nevertheless, I wondered if that was enough to satisfy this key way in which Jenna felt important. She clearly loved her job, but I had the strong sense that something was missing.

After working with Jenna for a short while, I realized that she was indeed longing for the chance to work more directly on creative projects—specifically, the painting that she had studied in college and that she had pursued quite seriously for a few years.

"I gave it up because I hated how competitive the art world was," she told me, "and because I knew I could never make a living at it." When I asked her whether she might want to maintain this side of her life even if it didn't produce any income, she shrugged. "Those kinds of dreams are for kids," she said. "I don't believe in that stuff anymore—I've grown up."

Jenna was simply denying that she felt a conflict between her aspects of importance of serving and of being creative. In effect, she was ignoring her own emotional fingerprint, insisting that one aspect of that fingerprint, being creative, didn't matter.

The price Jenna paid for denying her conflict was a growing sense of unhappiness that she couldn't quite name. She had started to feel that even her teaching was not as satisfying as it once was. She felt blocked in her relationships, telling me that none of the men she met were "interesting" or "exciting." I wondered whether she was looking to them to provide the creative side of her life and then becoming disappointed when they couldn't do so.

I also wondered whether Jenna's blocked creativity was keeping a more creative man from being interested in her. After all, if she couldn't support her own creative aspect, how could a potential life partner expect Jenna to support his creativity? Denying her conflicts meant that Jenna wasn't validating *any* aspect of her emotional fingerprint as fully as she could—which meant that ultimately she did not own her life.

I've had many other clients who made the same mistake. Roger, for example, was a successful lawyer who was also the father of three small children. When Roger was growing up, his father was gone all the time. Roger's father was a traveling salesman who worked hard to support his family, but as a result his children rarely saw him. When I interviewed Roger, we discovered two aspects of importance of his emotional fingerprint: providing and being a good parent. I wondered whether these two aspects were in conflict for him.

Like Jenna, Roger denied his conflict. He kept insisting to me that he *was* being a good parent by working hard, just as his own father had done, because that was the best way to help his children. Nevertheless, little remarks that he made led me to wonder whether he wasn't also feeling a gap in his life.

For example, once he said, "My wife, Alicia, is great with the kids, but sometimes she gets too wrapped up in their problems. I think if I were around more, it would give everybody some perspective." Then he quickly added, "Of course, I have to put in the time at work now. But maybe in a few years, when things lighten up . . . "

Another time he mentioned a trip that Alicia and the kids had taken to a local theme park. "I would really have loved to see Brian on his first roller coaster," he said wistfully. "That kid is fearless! I bet he just couldn't get enough of that ride." I saw in his eyes how proud he was of his son and how much he loved him. Then it was as though a steel gate had come down, blocking all of the emotion from Roger's face. "But of course, I had to work," he said, almost mechanically. "Work comes first."

Like Jenna, Roger was deeply committed to insisting that there was no conflict. As with Jenna, however, I could see that he was paying a price. He felt a general sense of dissatisfaction and described being taken over by a kind of "blah" feeling, in which even the things that he used to enjoy didn't give him much pleasure anymore. He told me that he frequently snapped at his wife and was almost always too tired to play with his kids even when he was home. It was almost as though, since he couldn't be with them very often, he couldn't bear to be with them at all; as though he had to shut down all of the emotions he felt around his children because it was too painful to miss them as much as he did. The conflict he didn't want to face was sapping the joy from his life.

Ignoring Your Emotional Fingerprint: Dishonoring Your Limits

When Jenna finally acknowledged that she was facing a conflict, she still insisted that she couldn't do anything about it. She told me that she couldn't make time for her painting because too many other people depended on her. She invoked her aspects of serving and of being needed to explain why she had to do everything possible for her students as well as do the grocery shopping for her widowed mother, help her brother care for his sick wife, and pitch in to care for her sister's four kids. Jenna was also active in her church, which validated her aspect of being connected to God, spirit, or the universe. She was constantly getting calls for help from neighbors and friends, which validated her aspect of being a friend.

All of these other pulls on her energy and time—work, family, church, neighbors, friends—made Jenna feel as though she had no right to any limits. She certainly did not feel comfortable saying no to others for as trivial a reason as "selfishly" validating her aspect of being creative. It was as though Jenna thought she had no right to set any limits—that whenever someone needed her, she was supposed to give unconditionally, completely, and without stopping, until that person gave her permission to stop. The limits were always set by other people at their convenience, never by Jenna at hers.

Jenna thought that she was following her emotional compass, which directed her to "Meet everyone else's needs before you even think about your own." I've found that a lot of women struggle with this kind of emotional compass, including my generous and loving wife, who is extremely devoted to her family and who frequently has trouble setting limits with both her natal family and her husband and children to make sure she has some breathing room for herself.

I salute such women for their generous spirits, but I think they should remember the warning on the airplane: put on your own oxygen mask before assisting others. If you aren't getting the air you need to breathe, you won't have what you need to help others.

If you aren't getting what you need to stay healthy and balanced, you won't be able to share your life with other people in a free and open way. If you aren't honoring your limits—deciding what you need, how much you can do, and when you will say no—you are ultimately ignoring your emotional fingerprint.

Remember, your emotional fingerprint has seven aspects, and all of them need to be validated. Not honoring your limits means that you are not taking responsibility for validating all seven aspects of your emotional fingerprint. In fact, you are validating other people's emotional fingerprints at the expense of your own.

What happens when you don't validate your emotional fingerprint? As we have seen in the previous chapters, not validating your emotional fingerprint means that you are out of balance with yourself. You aren't in control of your emotional ups and downs. You aren't making conscious, effective decisions about what kind of life you want. You're just drifting along, not even close to owning your life.

Moreover, if you aren't validating your emotional fingerprint, you are also not internalizing it. Owning your life means finding internal ways to validate your emotional fingerprint—approaches that you control, so that you are always in charge of your own happiness. Of course, you can seek external relationships with other people and external success in the world, but your foundation for those activities will be far stronger if you find an internal basis for them: an internalized emotional fingerprint that enables you to get all of your aspects of importance validated, regardless of how anyone else behaves.

When you're not honoring your limits, you will find it much harder to internalize your emotional fingerprint. Almost by definition, dishonoring your limits comes from focusing too much on other people: what they want from you, what they think of you, how they'd like you to act. If you're following their ideas at the expense of your own, how will you ever truly internalize your emotional fingerprint?

There's a paradox, however. If you don't honor your limits, you'll ultimately find it almost impossible to really help someone or to keep helping people over an extended period. Burnout, frustration, envy, resentment, and simple exhaustion are likely to get in your way. Remember the rule about putting on your own oxygen mask before assisting others. Without internalizing your emotional fingerprint and validating all of your aspects of importance, you will find it difficult to go the extra mile, to see the new possibilities for helping others, and to share a genuine spirit of joy and acceptance.

When you internalize your emotional fingerprint, as we saw in the previous chapter, you'll discover new emotional reserves that will enable you to be more generous, work harder, handle obstacles better, and extend yourself further. You will become a bigger, more expansive, more generous person who can do more for yourself and for the other people in your life. This process relies on honoring your limits so that you can take responsibility for validating your emotional fingerprint. Otherwise, your emotional reserves are likely to shrink instead of grow, as the pressures of life get to you and wear you down.

Jenna told me that she sometimes felt burned out at work. She was finding it increasingly difficult to be patient with her students' parents and even with the students themselves. She was also losing her temper with her family and her friends more often, which disturbed her a great deal.

Not validating her aspect of being creative was causing every other aspect of Jenna's emotional fingerprint to suffer. She wasn't living up to her own ideals of serving and being a friend. She was feeling burdened rather than nourished by being needed. She was even feeling less inspired than usual by her time in church.

Jenna insisted that she was genuinely committed to serving, being needed, connecting to God through her church, and being a good friend. She was, but by not validating her aspect of importance of being creative, she was throwing her entire system out of balance. By not honoring her own limits, she was weakening her ability to care for others as well as herself. She was not protecting her emotional fingerprint, and now she was paying the price.

Roger had his own way of dishonoring his limits. No matter what came up, he simply tried to work harder. When his wife got sick the same week that a new client showed up in town, Roger felt a conflict among several aspects of his emotional fingerprint: being in control, providing (both at home and at work), being a good parent, and honoring his standards (as husband, father, worker, and man).

Rather than honoring his limits in this difficult situation, Roger tried to fulfill both sets of responsibilities at the same time. He spent long hours in meetings with the new client, then came home late and got up early to take care of all of the household duties that his wife hadn't been able to do. As a result, he was frayed and exhausted at work, and he didn't make the good impression on the new client that he had hoped for. With his wife sick, he was forced to spend more time with his kids that week, but the time was all about pushing them to get their own work done: overseeing their homework and scolding them for not completing their chores. Roger was disappointed that his kids hadn't met his standards, and he was upset that he hadn't met his own standards. At the end of the week, everyone was exhausted, frustrated, and miserable.

It didn't occur to Roger to set limits at work in order to be home more or to set limits at home by asking family, friends, or even paid help to take care of the extra work at home. It didn't occur to him that during this difficult week, maybe he could relax his standards for what he, his wife, and the kids were supposed to do—that maybe this was the time to cut everybody some slack and just try to get through things as best they could. Instead, Roger tried to validate his aspects of importance of being in control, providing, being a good parent, and honoring his own standards by trying to do everything at the highest possible level, just as though there were no conflicts.

As a result, Roger ended up feeling that he had done nothing well. He spent the entire week feeling out of control, worrying about not providing enough either at home or at work, yelling at his kids, and regretting that he had not lived up to his superhuman standards. Not honoring his limits had not helped Roger resolve the conflicting aspects of his emotional fingerprint. It had only made things worse.

Honoring Your Limits

1. Identify three recent occasions on which you did not honor your limits. You might think of a time that you said yes even though you wished you could say no, or an incident in which you ended up helping someone else instead of doing something that you needed to do for yourself. You might also think of a situation in which someone talked you into doing something you now regret:

    a. _____

    b. _____

    c. _____

2. Now identify which aspects of importance of your emotional fingerprint you disrespected or failed to validate each time you dishonored your limits:

    a. _____

    b. _____

    c. _____

3. What were the consequences each time you dishonored your limits?

    a. _____

    b. _____

    c. _____

Externalizing Your Emotional Fingerprint: Seeking External Validation

As noted in chapter 4, when you seek external validation, you doom yourself to frustration, envy, resentment, disappointment, and low self-esteem. That's because sooner or later, you're going to find yourself unable to control the results, and you'll realize that your happiness is outside your control. Sometimes, no matter how hard you try, another person chooses not to return your love, an enterprise doesn't succeed, or your children don't turn out the way you planned. You just can't control all of the people and situations you come in contact with, so if you depend on them for validation, you will fail.

Seeking to have your emotional fingerprint validated by others is an exhausting and fruitless experience. It reminds me of a greyhound that runs on a track for hours chasing a mechanical rabbit but never catches it. In the same way, when people receive external validation, they are only left wanting more. No matter how often you are praised, reassured, or externally successful, you always have to worry about the next time. What if the praise runs out? What if the reassuring person changes his or her mind? What if the next time you aren't able to achieve what you did before? It's like the Hollywood saying "You're only as good as your last picture." No matter how great your success, failure always threatens.

Do you know someone who is never satisfied, no matter how many times you tell him that you think he's wonderful? Or someone who never seems happy, no matter what you do for her? Is there someone you know who seems to always be fishing for a compliment or says things just to get your attention? No matter what you do for these people, it is never enough. Trying to validate your emotional fingerprint externally is like having a bucket full of holes. The more you fill it, the more that flows out. You end up exhausted and emptied.

In contrast, when you internalize your emotional fingerprint, you feel satisfied, generous, grateful, enthusiastic, and self-confident. That's because you know that your happiness is within your control. By finding internal ways to validate your emotional fingerprint, you can ensure that you are always successful. It's like the old saying "If you go within, you'll never go without." It's as though the greyhound on the track stopped running after the mechanical rabbit, sat down, and turned around. Suddenly, instead of chasing the rabbit, all the dog has to do is sit there and wait for the rabbit to come around the track, rushing straight toward the greyhound.

Jenna and Roger were both still chasing the rabbit. As Jenna tried to resolve the conflict between her two aspects of importance, she was constantly comparing herself to other people and wondering how they managed to be so much more successful than she was. Her friend Natalie, from art school, had continued painting and was producing work that Jenna admired. Natalie had sold only a few pieces and was still supporting herself by working as a secretary, but Jenna envied her friend's ability to stick with something that she herself had given up on.

Jenna also compared herself unfavorably to her sister, Courtney. As soon as Courtney graduated from college, she married her childhood sweetheart, bought a home, and started having children. In Jenna's eyes, Courtney was the perfect wife and mother. Jenna believed that unlike herself, Courtney was always generous, patient, and unselfish, giving tirelessly to her family, her friends, and her church.

Jenna also knew people from art school who seemed to have done it all. Although she wasn't in touch with them anymore, she still read about them in the alumni newsletter and heard about them from Natalie. These men and women seemed to have become successful in every domain: marriage, children, and career. They even gave money to charity and participated in fundraisers for good causes.

When Jenna compared herself to these other people, she felt sure that she could never resolve her own conflict. "I'm not creative like Natalie—now there's someone who really had talent and stuck with it," she told me. Or "You should see what a good person my sister is. I'm nothing like her." Or "I know other people who manage to be creative *and* to do everything else, too. I guess you have to be born that way—or maybe they're just really lucky. I don't know. I just know I can't do what they do."

By externalizing her emotional fingerprint, Jenna was doomed to failure. She was simply never going to be as creative as Natalie, as unselfish as Courtney, or as successful as her old classmates from art school. How could she be? If she defined her goals in terms of what other people had accomplished—or, as seen from the outside, what they *seemed* to have accomplished—she would never be able to define her own success in terms that only Jenna could accomplish. Like the greyhound chasing the mechanical rabbit, she would never catch the success she was chasing. She would never resolve her conflict simply by imitating the way other people resolved theirs. If Jenna wanted to resolve her conflict, she would have to look within.

Roger also looked outside himself for a solution to his conflict. Although he was willing to work very hard to validate all of his aspects of importance, he still defined them in external terms. Validating his aspects of providing and being a good parent meant providing lots of financial support to his children and having them behave like model citizens who always worked hard and never screwed up. As a result, whenever one of his kids had trouble of any kind, Roger believed that he had failed as a parent. His only solution was to push his kids harder and to put in more hours at work to earn more money for what he thought they needed: tutors, after-school programs, a more expensive school.

Likewise, validating his aspects of importance of being in control and honoring his standards meant having everything in his life go just the way Roger thought it should. Consequently, whenever anything went wrong—a broken appliance, a sick wife, a colleague who made a bad decision—Roger felt out of control and as though he had failed. His solution was, once again, to push himself even harder—which only made him feel even more of a failure. Like the greyhound, Roger ran faster and faster, but he could never catch the mechanical rabbit, and he couldn't resolve his conflicts.

Protecting Your Emotional Fingerprint

It's nearly impossible to resolve your conflicts in a happy, productive way unless you protect your emotional fingerprint. You might find a temporary solution, even one that works for a few years. Eventually, though, not protecting your emotional fingerprint is likely to lead to frustration and burnout. In my opinion, protecting your emotional fingerprint is definitely a better way to go.

What does this look like in practice? Protecting your emotional fingerprint involves three key steps:

- Acknowledge the conflicts that are part of your emotional fingerprint.
- Honor the limits that are part of your emotional fingerprint.
- Internalize your emotional fingerprint by finding internal rather than external ways to validate it.

Acknowledge Your Conflicts

You can't resolve a conflict unless you take responsibility for all of the conflicting aspects of importance of your emotional fingerprint. If you don't acknowledge that your aspect of being a good parent is at odds with your aspect of being in control, or that your aspect of being free and independent is at odds with your aspect of being in a loving relationship, you will have a much harder time finding a solution to the conflict that takes every aspect of your emotional fingerprint into account. You're likely to suppress some parts of your emotional fingerprint, which usually leads to a loss of joy and vitality. You may choose solutions to your conflict that won't really satisfy you in the long run. Then you might always feel a nagging sense of loss and regret, wondering if there was a better way.

In contrast, if you resolve conflicts with full awareness of your emotional fingerprint, you're far more likely to find a solution that really satisfies you, because it takes every part of yourself into account. Even if you make a compromise or choose to prioritize one aspect of your emotional fingerprint over another, doing so consciously and with full awareness of your emotional fingerprint means that you will wholeheartedly embrace the compromise and feel that it is the best possible solution.

Think of the aspects of importance of your emotional fingerprint as citizens in a democracy, where everyone is supposed to receive equal respect. Now suppose that this democracy has to make a difficult decision, involving some kind of compromise for its members. If this decision is made without a full discussion, with everyone getting to have his or her say, some members of the group might feel slighted and resentful. They'll have a hard time getting behind the new decision, especially if it's less favorable to them.

If everyone in the group talks things through so that everyone understands the problem and all of the available solutions, then when the group reaches a decision, everyone will be on board. They'll all be able to accept the compromise—even if they have to sacrifice a bit—because the group made the compromise consciously and with the full participation of every member.

In the same way, when you have to choose one aspect of your emotional fingerprint over another, you are far more likely to be successful if you have acknowledged every aspect and at least *tried* to validate all of them. This is a conscious lifestyle change that makes you more successful and happy. It is not a onetime event but rather a better, more efficient way to live.

I have certainly struggled with these issues, even very recently. When I was writing this book, for example, I had to meet many deadlines that caused conflicts within my emotional fingerprint. Although finishing the book met my life's purpose, was one way for me to provide for my family, and was part of being creative, it also put me in conflict with being a good parent, feeling free and independent, and experiencing life. I did not have enough time to spend with my children, and I often felt tied down by obligations.

I did not always handle these conflicts successfully, but when I remembered to honor my limits, I found ways to protect my emotional fingerprint and compromises I could live with.

One thing I did was to set aside fifteen-minute pockets of time to play with my kids. Even if I couldn't be with them as much as the good parent in me wanted to be, I didn't give up time with them altogether, and I vowed to make every single minute with them count.

I also set aside six to eight o'clock every evening to have dinner with my family, and I refused to work on Sunday so I could be with them. I would work from eight to midnight every night in order to preserve those other times. It wasn't a perfect solution, but it was definitely a good one.

Likewise, things started to get better for both Jenna and Roger when they acknowledged their conflicts honestly. When Jenna admitted how much her aspect of importance of being creative was not being met and how much she missed painting, she had taken the first step to figuring out how to resolve her conflict in a satisfying and productive way. When Roger came to terms with how much he missed spending time with his kids and how sad it made him to see them so rarely, he had opened the door to a better solution. Acknowledging your conflicts while being aware of every aspect of importance is crucial to protecting your emotional fingerprint.

EXERCISE

Acknowledging Your Conflicts

1. Choose one of the conflicts from the "Identifying Your Conflicts" exercise.
2. Look at the aspects of importance that you identified as being in conflict. Take a moment to consider whether you would identify any new aspects in the situation and whether you now see the conflict in a new way.
3. For each aspect you have identified, write two or three sentences expressing what you would need for this aspect of importance to be satisfied. Don't worry about whether what you're writing seems possible or whether there are contradictions in it.

Use this example of Roger as a guide:

Conflict: Wishing I could spend more time with my kids but needing to earn a living to provide for them.

Aspects of my emotional fingerprint in conflict: Providing versus being a good parent.

> Providing: I want to make sure I give my kids everything they need to have a good life. I want to earn enough money for them to go to the best schools and to do everything they want later on. I want to have a financial cushion so that even if something goes wrong, I can provide for them.

Being a good parent: I want my kids to have everything they need financially. But I also wish I could spend more time with them. I'd love to take them to theme parks and watch them have fun going on rides. I'd love to just hang out with them and have a good time, instead of seeing them only when they're tired and I'm tired, and always having to get on them about homework and chores.

Now it's your turn.

Conflict:

_____

Aspects of my emotional fingerprint in conflict:

_____

_____

Honor Your Limits

As we have seen, honoring your limits is a crucial part of protecting your emotional fingerprint. It can be tempting to act like Superman or Wonder Woman, as if you were capable of doing everything you wished you could do. It can be hard to say no or to limit what you do, especially when the requests come from people you love or when you see that someone you care about is in need. If you don't protect your emotional fingerprint, however, you'll end up drained and depleted, unable to help anyone as much as you'd like and paying a huge personal price in physical, mental, emotional, and spiritual exhaustion.

To honor your limits, you have to continually do three things:

- Check in with your emotional fingerprint and see whether any aspects of it are being disrespected.
- Identify which elements of a situation are within your control and which are outside your control.
- Decide which elements in a situation are your responsibility and which are not.

Here's how the process worked for Jenna. She had decided to check out a summer art program, and she had put aside a precious free afternoon to look through some catalogs and course descriptions online. She was interrupted, though, by a frantic call from her sister Courtney, who wondered whether Jenna could come over and watch the kids.

"I've canceled this hair appointment three times," Courtney said breathlessly, "and I have to go out with Patrick tonight to meet some people from his job, and I really *can't* go looking like this. I promised the kids that I'd take them to the movies—they've been at me about it all week—and they really miss you, and they'd love to see you. Would you be willing to take them?"

"Why can't Patrick do it?" Jenna asked.

"Oh, he's got something planned, and I hate to ask him—he works so hard all week, and this is his one free day. And the kids were asking me just the other night why they don't see their aunt Jenna anymore, so what do you say?"

Normally, Jenna would have felt flattered, guilty, and genuinely happy about seeing her nieces and nephews. She would have felt sorry for Courtney and Patrick, who worked hard at their jobs and at their parenting, and she would have been glad to do her sister a favor.

Now she still felt all of those things—but she also realized how much she had been looking forward to validating at least a little of her creative aspect. She acknowledged her conflict, thinking, "At this moment, my creative aspect of my emotional fingerprint is in conflict with my aspects of being needed and serving." Being aware of the conflict helped Jenna to remember that she had a responsibility to her creative aspect as much as to the aspects of serving and being needed.

Then she thought about her limits, saying to herself, "I can't always do everything. Sometimes there will be conflicts, and I'll have to decide which aspect is more important to me or what a good compromise might be." Trying to honor her limits rather than simply doing what her sister asked of her or deciding that her own needs weren't important, she realized how much she wanted to spend the afternoon focusing on her creative aspect of importance and how little she wanted to sacrifice that part of herself today.

Next, she thought about what she could and could not control. She thought, "I can't magically create an afternoon in which I can both look at the catalogs *and* take the kids to the movies. I can't figure out a way that Courtney can both get her hair done *and* take the kids to the movies. I don't even know what Patrick is doing, so I can't figure out *his* life." Jenna realized that it was not in her power to fix the whole problem. She could not come up with a solution in which she, Courtney, Patrick, and the kids would all get what they wanted. That simply wasn't in her control. All she could do was to make a compromise in which at least one person would be giving something up.

Finally, Jenna thought about what she was and was not responsible for. For perhaps the first time in her life, she decided that *she* was not going to be the person who gave something up. She thought, "Courtney's kids, her hairdresser, her dinner with Patrick's colleagues, and Patrick's busy schedule are not my responsibility. I didn't promise to take the kids to the movies today. I didn't schedule and break the hair appointments or make the plans with Patrick. This is Courtney's problem. I wish I could help her, but it's not my *responsibility* to help her. So I have a choice, and I choose to validate my creative aspect and let Courtney solve her own problems. Maybe she can find someone else to take the kids. Maybe she can find a way to fit everything in. Maybe she'll go out with her hair looking 'awful,' or cancel the dinner with Patrick's people, or find some solution I can't even imagine. I hope she works it out, but it's not my responsibility, and I'm going to say no."

When you set limits with people—especially with loved ones or colleagues who are used to you *not* honoring your limits—you are likely to run into some resistance. In this case, Courtney pulled out all the stops to try to talk Jenna into taking the kids. Normally that would have worked, but because Jenna had really gotten in touch with her emotional fingerprint and was determined to protect it, she was able to keep saying no to Courtney—a loving but very firm no.

She knew that she didn't want a relationship with Courtney that was based on not honoring her own limits. If Courtney loved her, she would support Jenna's right to have limits even while sometimes disagreeing with her about how they were set. If Courtney did not accept Jenna's right to set limits, their relationship might well suffer, but Jenna realized that she was willing to accept this possibility. Honoring her own limits had suddenly become important to her. *Sometimes* she would do what Courtney asked, sacrificing her own needs for those of her sister and her sister's kids, but not *every* time.

When Jenna hung up the phone and went to her computer, she felt a sense of peace that surprised her. Even though she hadn't yet resolved the biggest conflicts between her aspects of importance, she felt calm and confident, certain that a solution would be found even though she didn't yet know what it was. That's the reward for being aware of your emotional fingerprint, acknowledging conflicts, and honoring your limits. You almost always feel more hopeful and at peace. That's because you've just reminded yourself that you can trust yourself to protect your emotional fingerprint.

EXERCISE

Honoring Your Limits More

1. From the previous "Honoring Your Limits" exercise, choose one of the occasions on which you did not honor your limits.

2. Remind yourself which aspects of importance of your emotional fingerprint you disrespected or failed to validate on that occasion. If you see the situation differently now, add or change some aspects.

3. Ask yourself what, in that situation, you could and could not control.

   Could control:

   _____

   _____

Could not control:

_____

_____

4. Ask yourself what, in that situation, you were and were not responsible for.

   Responsible for:

   _____

   _____

   Not responsible for:

   _____

   _____

5. Now think about what you might do the next time a similar situation arises. What might you want to do to honor your limits?

   _____

   _____

Internalize Your Emotional Fingerprint

When you're faced with a conflict between two (or more) aspects of your emotional fingerprint, it's always useful to see if there is any further way you can "go internal." Have you fully internalized your emotional fingerprint, or are you still looking to external relationships and results to validate some aspects of who you are?

Roger found that he had to work especially hard at internalizing his emotional fingerprint. All his life he had looked outward for validation and support. He looked to his wife to validate that he was a good father and husband, he looked to his kids to acknowledge that he was a good father ("Someday you'll appreciate me for making you do chores like this!"), and he looked to his clients, his colleagues, and his boss to respect his work and appreciate his high standards. Like Jenna, he set very high standards for himself and then measured himself against his ideas about other people.

All of Roger's externalizing put his emotional fingerprint at risk and depleted his emotional reserves. He couldn't think clearly about how to resolve the conflicts he was facing until he internalized his emotional fingerprint. No matter what happened in his relationships or at work, he was always in the driver's seat. This sense of power and responsibility was very liberating to Roger, and in a sense it freed him to honor his limits and make his own choices.

As a result, he made what for some would be a radical decision, but for Roger it was exactly the right choice. He asked his office to consider a flextime arrangement in which he would work at home two days a week. That way, he could get almost as much work done as before, but he could arrange his time to be available when his kids were awake and ready to talk, so he could spend better quality time with them.

Roger also decided that he would work on Saturday, if necessary, but not on Sunday. Even if he had to work late into the night

---

Resolving Conflicts by Protecting Your Emotional Fingerprint

Don't:
- Ignore your emotional fingerprint by denying that your conflicts exist
- Ignore your emotional fingerprint by dishonoring your limits
- Externalize your emotional fingerprint by comparing yourself unfavorably to others and seeking other forms of external validation

Do:
- Acknowledge the conflicts that are part of your emotional fingerprint
- Honor the limits that are part of your emotional fingerprint
- Internalize your emotional fingerprint by finding internal rather than external ways to validate it

after his kids were sleeping, he managed to be free during the day on Saturday and all day and night on Sunday. That way, he had big chunks of time to take his kids to a theme park, go to the beach with them, or just hang out. He had found a way to validate both the providing aspect of his emotional fingerprint and his aspect of being a good parent, and he had done it without denying the conflict, dishonoring his limits, or giving up any aspect of his emotional fingerprint.

We don't get to choose the circumstances of our lives, and to my knowledge, none of us has superpowers, but if you make your choices with awareness, honoring your limits and protecting your emotional fingerprint, you can say to yourself, "Sure, things aren't going my way right now, but at the end of the day, I'm happy with the choices I've made. The obstacles I've encountered may slow me down, but they won't stop me. I'll keep going until I've built the life I want."

Now that you know how to protect your emotional fingerprint, it's time to look at ways to strengthen it still further. In the next chapter, we'll look more closely at approaches for validating every aspect of importance of your emotional fingerprint.

6

Validate Your Emotional Fingerprint

Two men looked out from prison bars; one saw the mud, the other saw the stars.

—Frederick Langbridge

I f you looked at Drew Barrymore's early life, you would have thought she had it made. She was born into a family of brilliant actors, the heir to two generations of men and women who starred on stage and screen. At age one, she already had her first acting job, as a baby in a dog food commercial. At age seven, she became famous for playing the lovable sister, Gerti, in Steven Spielberg's *E.T.: The Extraterrestrial.*

There was nothing cute and lovable about her behavior just a few years later, however. Before Barrymore was even a teenager, she was a regular at the infamous Studio 54 and developed an addiction to drugs and alcohol. By age thirteen she was acting violently, in one instance trying to kick her mother out of their house. Eventually, after an attempted suicide, the child star was forced to go into rehab.

Barrymore tried to put her life and her acting career back on track, but she didn't really have the tools to do so. You might say that she was still seeking external validation for her emotional fingerprint, an effort that often runs aground. She tried to resurrect her shattered life, and she did manage to land some roles in a few movies, but those first steps back into the world of film were not successful because of her reputation as a problem child. No one was willing to believe that she had actually overcome her past.

Still seeking external validation for her emotional fingerprint, Barrymore got into one mess after another. At age nineteen, she married bar owner Jeremy Thomas and then ended the marriage three months later. She posed nude for *Playboy*. She even flashed her breasts to talk-show host David Letterman on national television.

Then, seemingly out of nowhere, Barrymore turned everything around by finding a new way to validate her emotional fingerprint. Instead of seeking external validation, she began to look within. Her emotional fingerprint itself hadn't changed, but her way of validating it had. Perhaps she had been inspired by something she learned in rehab or in counseling. Maybe she simply decided to change her life. However it happened, Barrymore's shift from external to internal validation expanded her emotional reserves exponentially. The fragile, unstable child star desperately seeking to be noticed and cared for became a strong, independent young woman with an artistic vision of her own.

With her newfound strength and resilience, she created her own production company, Flower Films, which produced the film that gave Barrymore her turnaround role, *Never Been Kissed*. Her company has become a huge success and has produced ten feature films, grossing more than $890 million.

Barrymore tapped into other strengths and became a successful model, acting as both the face of CoverGirl Cosmetics and a representative for Gucci Jewelry in 2007. The same year, she was selected number one on *People* magazine's annual "100 Most Beautiful People" list. She was named ambassador against hunger for the

United Nations World Food Program, a cause to which she has donated more than a million dollars. In 2010 she won a Golden Globe for her role in *Grey Gardens.*

"If you're going to go through hell . . . I suggest you come back learning something," Barrymore has said. "Life is very interesting . . . in the end, some of your greatest pains become your greatest strengths. I believe that everything happens for a reason, but I think it's important to seek out that reason—that's how we learn."

Barrymore went from being a troubled young woman with a drug addiction whom nobody in Hollywood wanted to work with to a powerful, centered, and well-respected actor and producer in control of her own artistic destiny. Her shift is inspiring, because it proves that anyone, at any stage of life, can make a change.

It also demonstrates that the internal validation of your emotional fingerprint can expand your emotional reserves a thousandfold. I see this as the clear moral to Barrymore's story. As the saying goes, once you learn how to truly go within, you'll never go without. Once you are practiced at validating your emotional fingerprint internally, you'll become more powerful and more effective, and opportunities will almost magically open up.

How do you make the shift from external to internal validation? The most effective way, in my experience, is through a process known as *reassociation.*

Association and Reassociation

An *association* is, quite simply, the connection we make between two things. Perhaps you smile when you hear a song from your past because you associate it with the summer you turned sixteen and the whole world seemed to be opening up. Perhaps I frown or wince when I hear the same song because I associate it with the girl who left me for my best friend at the high school dance, with the summer my grandmother died, or with how lonely and lost I felt as a teenager. Same song, different associations—and, as a result, different emotional responses and perhaps even different judgments (you think it's the best song ever; I think it's dull or unsatisfying).

Associations are powerful because, as the example shows, they are the vehicle for strong emotion. Do you associate warmth and comfort with the smell of baking bread, or do you recoil in horror, thinking, "I hate bread—too many calories"? Do you associate books with the excitement of learning something new, with the boredom of sitting through a difficult class and the annoying pretensions of people who are always showing off their fancy degrees, or with the wonder and mystery of a world you don't understand but would like to? Your association will determine your emotional response to books.

Reassociation is the act of making a conscious change or even a forced change in an association. If you love the smell of baking bread and then are abruptly told that you have diabetes and you'll have to avoid starchy food, your terror of the disease you've just developed may cause you to lose your appreciation for the smell of the once favorite food. If you enjoy driving fast in a car with the top down and then narrowly avoid a major accident, you may discover that you no longer like daredevil driving. You no longer associate bread with comfort or driving with adventure. Instead, you associate both items with danger, and your emotions shift accordingly.

Those are examples of *forced* reassociations, made when life circumstances make it imperative for you to create new associations. I recommend *conscious* reassociations.

My wife happens to be a master at reassociation, so let me illustrate the process of conscious reassociation by describing one of her masterstrokes. A few years ago, I got a call from my brother, a talented marketer who was filming a twelve-episode show about other acclaimed marketers. He invited me to sit in on an interview he was doing with a man I had long admired, a brilliant Internet marketer. I would have the opportunity to act as my brother's unpaid production assistant, a role that would give me the chance to hear several hours of conversation in which my brother pumped this entrepreneur for his marketing secrets. The program would eventually be edited down to a single hour, but by working on the production, I would have a front-row seat for the entire interview.

The only catch was that the interview was taking place in Atlanta and the invitation came at the last minute, so the only airline ticket I could get was for an extremely expensive first-class seat. If I wanted to travel from Los Angeles to Atlanta, I would have to spend more than fifteen hundred dollars. I just couldn't rationalize spending that kind of money on a plane ticket. Feeling sad, I prepared to call my brother and refuse his offer.

Then my wife stepped in. "Honey," she said, "this marketer that your brother is going to interview—he is someone you want to learn from and do business with, right?"

"Oh, yes," I answered. "I've followed his work for years."

"And if you go, you get to hear his best information for something like six or eight hours?"

"Yes, that's the idea. My brother is a great interviewer, so I'm sure he'll get this guy to really open up. And the man has already said he'll cooperate, so I know he'll have a lot to say."

"Well," my wife asked me, "would you be willing to spend fifteen hundred dollars for an exclusive all-day seminar with one of your marketing heroes?"

I was floored. If that had been the proposition, I would have snapped it up in a second. I believed that the information I was being given the chance to learn was worth several times the cost of the plane ticket. I picked up the phone and gave my brother an enthusiastic yes, and I marveled at the power of reassociation. When the fifteen hundred dollars was for a plane ticket, it was too expensive, but when it was the price of an exclusive seminar, it was almost too cheap. Changing my association of the fifteen hundred dollars from airline ticket to seminar had completely transformed my emotional response, and it allowed me to make an entirely different decision.

━━━━━━━━━━━━━━━━━━━━━ **E X E R C I S E** ━━━━━━━━━━━━━━━━━━━━━

Identifying and Transforming Your Associations

1. List five negative associations you have and the emotions that go with them. Be as specific as you can. Use the following example:

Item	Association	Emotion
1. Mother-in-law visiting	My mother-in-law will tell me what to do.	Resentment, contempt, anger
2. People asking me to lower my voice	Being thought loud and annoying	Embarrassed, resentful, frustrated, misunderstood
3. Working out	Too hard, not convenient	Painful, feel like a failure, feel undisciplined
4. Helping around the house	I've worked all day! Why should I have to work when I get home?	Unappreciated, overworked
5. Paying my bills	Overwhelmed, worried that I don't have more money	Frustrated, depressed, scared

Item	Association	Emotion
1. _____	_____	_____
2. _____	_____	_____
3. _____	_____	_____
4. _____	_____	_____
5. _____	_____	_____

2. Now choose from the list three items that you have trouble with. As my wife did with me, create a reassociation for each item that transforms your emotions from negative to positive. In the same example:

Item	Reassociation	Emotion
1. Mother-in-law visiting	She'll watch the kids, and my wife and I can have a night out! I'll be grateful to her.	Gratitude, relief

Item	Reassociation	Emotion
2. Working out	Instead of going to a boring gym, I will get back into cycling and spend more time outside. If I also eat healthier food, I will live longer and be able to help my children to have healthier habits.	Enthusiasm
3. Helping around the house	I love my job and would not want to trade places with anyone. I am free during the day to choose what I do with my time. When I come home, I will get everyone involved in helping to keep the house clean.	Gratitude

Item	Reassociation	Emotion
1. _____	_____	_____
2. _____	_____	_____
3. _____	_____	_____

Creating Internal Reassociations

My wife's brilliant reassociation was simply a new way of looking at something, but I suggest that you take things a step further, as Drew Barrymore did. I want to encourage you to reassociate from external to internal associations and to do so at every opportunity. This, I believe, is the fastest and most powerful way to expand your emotional reserves. By relentlessly discovering internal validations for every aspect of importance of your emotional fingerprint, you guarantee your own happiness, make effective decisions, agree to appropriate risks, and take a huge step on the path to owning your life.

Here is an example of what I mean. Suppose you are considering a switch from your current job to becoming an entrepreneur. You're going to start small, beginning your business while still working at your old job, but if things go well, your plan is to be self-employed by the end of the year.

If you consider such a move, how would you define your success? Most people would answer that question in terms of external results. They would define success as earning a lot of money, being able to leave the old job, or becoming financially secure. Anything else they would deem a failure.

The problem with this approach is that it puts them at the mercy of life circumstances. The financial success of your enterprise is not completely up to you. An unexpected event, such as an economic downturn or a natural disaster, could devastate your business overnight. Are you then a failure? An externalized set of associations would make you believe that you are.

What if you defined success internally? What if you defined it in terms of internally validating aspects of your emotional fingerprint, regardless of the outcome of your efforts?

You might say, for example, that the business was a success if it allowed you to validate your aspect of importance of being creative or if it allowed you to become free and independent, at least temporarily. Perhaps the mere act of starting the business validates your aspect of overcoming challenges, being in control, working, or providing.

Seeing your actions in terms of how well you have internally validated your emotional fingerprint—something over which you have complete control—gives you power over your destiny. Seeing yourself this way often requires you to change your associations. Suppose your business does fail. Internalizing your emotional fingerprint and validating it for yourself means giving up your focus on the financial failure of the business and all of the hardship that this might entail for you and your family.

Instead, you would focus on your own courage and determination as you battled to realize your dream. You would feel successful based on how well you conducted yourself or how you kept battling on even after you acted badly or made mistakes. Although your enterprise might be in ruins, you would take away a new image of what you're capable of. The emotional reserves that you'd build by seeing yourself this way would give you a chance to take a deep breath and start another business.

This is not a rah-rah "power of positive thinking" speech. I had two failed businesses before I started my current, very successful coaching practice, and I know how painful, frightening, and disheartening financial failure can be. In my multivolume study of successful entrepreneurs, I was struck by the truth of the old boxing adage: It's not how many times you're knocked down that counts, it's how many times you get up. As I was studying the lives of successful men and women, I was amazed at how many failures each of them had weathered, how many seemingly insuperable obstacles each had faced, how many crushing disappointments each had experienced.

Later, I realized that their experience was equally true of writers, artists, politicians, and scientists. Most great figures in their fields have encountered failures that less ambitious souls can scarcely imagine. Their willingness to keep getting up after they were repeatedly knocked down is what made them great.

Consider the story of R. H. Macy, who founded the landmark Macy's department store, which would ultimately become one of the world's leading retail chains. Macy actually failed four times before he succeeded—spectacularly—the fifth time. He started a store in Boston in 1844 that went out of business soon after it opened, then founded a dry goods store that failed about two years later, after Macy had spent months trying to keep it going. In 1849, he went to California in the midst of the gold rush, but even those boom times did not save Macy's third business, which failed as well. Macy gave the retail business a fourth try, but this latest venture, a store in Haverhill, Massachusetts, went bankrupt as well.

After four unsuccessful attempts at running a store, Macy somehow found the courage to try yet a fifth time. The fifth time was the charm: the New York store that grew rapidly to become the largest in the world and dominate America's idea of the department store for many decades.

What makes someone like Macy able to keep starting businesses even after so many go under? What makes a scientist able to keep coming back to a problem even after several experiments fail? What makes a politician able to run again for public office even after several lost elections?

There are many possible answers. People may be driven by an overwhelming need for revenge, personal power, or individual glory. They may be so hungry for external validation that they won't turn back, no matter what obstacles they encounter. If they are driven by the need for external validation—as the young Drew Barrymore was—they won't be happy no matter how much they achieve. No matter what triumphs they accomplish, they will never be satisfied or feel complete. Like the greyhound on the racetrack, they're going to keep chasing after a mechanical rabbit that always somehow eludes them, no matter what achievements they've managed to rack up.

If, like the more mature and accomplished Barrymore, they redefine their notions of success based on an internal validation of their emotional fingerprints, they'll feel a sense of accomplishment and satisfaction at every step of the journey, and they'll have the resilience to keep going through all of the ups and downs.

If this is true in your work life, it will be equally true in your relationships and your personal life. If you define success in these areas in terms of an external goal—getting married, having friends, living in a pleasant environment—then your happiness is contingent on external circumstances. If the marriage breaks up, the friends move away, or the environment changes, you're back to square one, and where do you then find the emotional reserves to start over?

If you define your relationships by your role as a loving person rather than by the response you get from a particular partner, and if you define your personal life by the way you conduct yourself rather than by the results you achieve, your happiness will always be within your grasp. Moreover, you'll find that you're much more able to receive validation, praise, respect, trust, and love from others, because you're already giving these things to yourself.

If you know that you're dependent on a partner's validation, you'll find it far more difficult to enjoy that partner, even when things are going well. The shadow of losing the other person, whether through divorce or death, will always be present, reminding you of how vulnerable you are. If you know that you'll always be loved and validated, with or without that partner, you have the freedom to enjoy whatever the person chooses to give you and to savor it to the fullest. That's how you can expand your emotional fingerprint and own your life.

EXERCISE

Learning to Reassociate

I suggest that you repeat this exercise every day until it becomes second nature and you find that you are doing it automatically. When aspects of importance of your emotional fingerprint are being disrespected by external circumstances, you can use the process modeled by this exercise to change your focus from external validations that you cannot control to internal validations that you can control. Once you reassociate from external to internal validations, you have taken your life back into your hands.

1. Choose a specific time this week that you felt depressed, angry, or frustrated.
2. Identify which aspects of your emotional fingerprint were disrespected.
3. For each aspect you identified, name something you can do to validate that aspect internally.

For example:

Negative Experience	Aspect Disrespected	Reassociation (Internal Validation)
Kids fought all day	Being a good parent	My definition of being a good parent means that the kids will fight sometimes. What can I teach them about conflict resolution? How can I practice patience? What positive aspects of my kids come out when they fight?

(continued)

Negative Experience	Aspect Disrespected	Reassociation (Internal Validation)
Lost a lifelong friend	Being a friend	This loss came from my personal growth; I grew, and my friend did not grow with me. How will my other friendships benefit from my growth?
Got laid off	Providing, being secure, working	I will find ways to provide emotionally and spiritually for my family, regardless of finances. I will find security in my ability to meet challenges rather than in a job or a circumstance. I will work at finding a new job or creating new economic opportunities and will also do volunteer work in my community.

Negative Experience	Aspect Disrespected	Reassociation (Internal Validation)
_____	_____	_____ _____
_____	_____	_____ _____
_____	_____	_____ _____

Creating Internal Validations

You've seen how valuable it can be to create internal validations for every aspect of importance of your emotional fingerprint. You may still need some help imagining what an internal validation looks like, so to get you started with your own creation of internal validations, here are ten suggestions for validating each aspect of your emotional fingerprint.

Not all of these ideas will work for everybody, and you'll certainly want to come up with your own approaches for validating your emotional fingerprint, but at least some of these ideas may inspire you.

Group 1

I feel important when I am in control.

1. Master your mind, your body, and your soul.
2. Set standards for living that are within your control (see chapter 7 for more on defining standards rather than expectations).
3. Acknowledge what you cannot control. Let other people have control.
4. Organize your personal life, your home, and your business.
5. Get rid of any clutter in your life.
6. Make a list of ten things you control.
7. Let go of what you cannot control.
8. Apologize to anyone you have tried to control.
9. Set measurable and obtainable goals.
10. Slow down and meditate, pray, do conscious breathing, practice yoga or tai chi, or find some other way to center yourself.

I feel important when I am confident in my appearance.

1. Let go of any negative self-images and replace them with things you like about yourself.
2. Express gratitude for the way you look, act, and feel.
3. Go shopping for new clothes.
4. Study current fashions.
5. Wear an outfit that you have been saving for a special occasion.
6. Find and embrace your unique style.
7. Treat yourself to something new.
8. Pamper yourself at a spa or get a massage.

9. Write down five things you like about yourself. Keep the list visible or handy so that you remember the items often.

10. Organize your closet and see if you can discover some hidden treasures.

I feel important when I am organized.

1. Use a planner or make to-do lists whose items you can cross off as you accomplish them.

2. Let go of what you cannot organize, such as other people or environments that are out of your control.

3. Organize the garage or some other storage space.

4. Focus on organizing your life and not the lives of others.

5. Read a book or search the Web for suggestions on how to be more organized.

6. Organize your time so that you will feel free.

7. Clean out a closet.

8. Make three piles when organizing: keep, throw away, and sell or donate.

9. Whether for income or as a volunteer, teach a class on how to be more organized.

10. Make organizing fun by involving other people.

I feel important when I am connected to God, spirit, or the universe.

1. Pray or meditate.

2. Create and use affirmations.

3. Repent or ask forgiveness for any wrong you've committed. Depending on the circumstances, you can ask others, your idea of God, or yourself for forgiveness.

4. Forgive others.

5. Practice charity.

6. Spend time in nature.

7. Read a religious or an inspirational book that connects you to your beliefs.

8. Study different religions.

9. Designate a time to be connected to God, spirit, or the universe for fifteen, thirty, or sixty minutes each day.

10. Let go and accept that God, spirit, or the universe is in control.

I feel important when I am trusted.

1. Remember that the more you trust yourself, the more others will put their trust in you.

2. Trust your instincts.

3. Live your life to be worthy of others' trust.

4. Forgive yourself and others for any wrongdoings or breaches of trust.

5. Live with integrity.

6. Stand for something.

7. Have character.

8. Define your standards and live by them (for more on standards, see chapter 7).

9. Trust yourself to make the right decisions.

10. Study the lives of people who were trusted with responsibility.

Group 2

I feel important when I am providing.

1. Study financial magazines and books.

2. Join an investment club.

3. Plan for retirement.

4. Start a business.

5. Look for a better job.

6. Save more money.

7. Consolidate your debt.

8. Remember that providing is not only financial; provide emotional, physical, spiritual, and mental support to those who need it.

9. Have a garage sale so you can provide others with what you no longer need while providing yourself with some extra cash.

10. Hire a financial planner or strategist.

I feel important when I am overcoming challenges.

1. Let go of something in your past that has bothered you.
2. Set obtainable goals to benefit your mind or body.
3. Set strategic goals to accomplishing a particular desire.
4. Acknowledge your past challenges as triumphs by identifying what you learned from them and how you have grown from them.
5. Read inspiring books and magazines about your power to overcome challenges or about others who have done so.
6. Help others to overcome obstacles.
7. Write a story, a song, or a poem about beating the odds.
8. Become a mentor.
9. Volunteer at a shelter, a food bank, or a charity so you can help others overcome their obstacles in a particular, concrete way.
10. Celebrate your life now by listing all of the challenges you have overcome to become exactly who you are right now.

I feel important when I am in the moment.

1. Just breathe. Take a moment to just relax and breathe.
2. Take time for yourself.
3. Pray or meditate.
4. Go for a walk.
5. Let go of negative energy by focusing on the positive elements of your life.
6. Express gratitude for what you have now in the moment.

7. Listen to calming music.

8. Learn to play a musical instrument.

9. Pamper yourself.

10. Play! Play a game or a sport and just play.

I feel important when I am in a loving relationship.

1. If you are single, be a little more outgoing and flirtatious. If you are in a committed relationship, be even more flirtatious with your partner.

2. If you are single, reach out to your friends to introduce you to someone. If you are in a relationship, pretend that you have just met your partner and discover something new about him or her.

3. Let go of grudges, anger, and negative thoughts.

4. Pamper yourself—and your partner, if you have one.

5. If you're in a relationship, designate time each week to spend with your partner. If you are single, designate time each week for relationships: to meet someone, to prepare yourself to meet someone, or to become more loving and better at relating.

6. Express gratitude for all of your relationships: romances, family members, friends, neighbors, community.

7. Read books that support having a healthy relationship.

8. If you're in a relationship, give yourself time off from relationship building to just play and have fun. If you're single, give yourself time off from relationship seeking to just play and have fun.

9. If you are single, try an Internet dating service. If you're in a relationship, look on the Internet for resources that can deepen your relationship: articles, workshops, couples' retreats.

10. If you are in a relationship, honor and respect your commitment to each other. If you are single, honor and respect all of your relationship commitments: to family, friends, neighbors, and colleagues.

I feel important when I am given respect.

1. Remember that you are the only one who can give you the respect you need and deserve. Focus on ways to respect yourself.
2. Get out of or change any relationship with a person who does not respect you.
3. Let go of anything—past or present—that causes you to respect yourself less.
4. Respect differences in others.
5. Set your standards and live by them.
6. Be worthy of respect, but don't demand it; earn it.
7. Have respect for your past and understand how it has brought you to where you are.
8. Study such virtues as integrity, honor, valor, and commitment.
9. Lend a hand to someone in need. Show yourself that you can respect someone who needs help as well as someone who offers it.
10. Respect who you are by acknowledging the positive decisions you have made in your life.

Group 3

I feel important when I am working.

1. Start a business.
2. Organize your work or home space.
3. Read books or articles with suggestions for working more effectively.
4. Create or join a mastermind (a group that helps one another with a certain topic) at work.
5. Set goals for your work and make a plan for how to meet them.
6. Reward yourself for working.
7. Educate yourself to increase your value in the workplace.

8. Become a mentor to a young entrepreneur or junior professional in your field.

9. Participate in micro loans to other countries so you can help others to work.

10. Study the lives of great innovators and entrepreneurs.

I feel important when I am free and independent.

1. Create time for yourself.

2. Create a master plan for how you can feel independent in your life.

3. Lend a voice to those who are too weak to stand on their own.

4. Write your own declaration of independence or mission statement.

5. Start something new: a hobby, a project, a course of study, or an adventure.

6. Pamper yourself with a little trinket or a spa treatment.

7. Skydive, scuba dive, climb a mountain, or paraglide.

8. Create a list of all of your previous accomplishments.

9. Meditate to create inner freedom.

10. Help someone who is not expecting your help.

I feel important when I am relying on my knowledge.

1. Find lists of critics' picks for best books of all time and read the books on the lists.

2. Memorize ten new points of interest on your favorite topic.

3. Take a course at a local college.

4. Take an online course.

5. Share your knowledge by teaching.

6. Learn another language.

7. Study a new topic.

8. Learn about other cultures, businesses, or religions.

9. Create a website about your favorite area of knowledge.

10. Write a book on your life experiences.

I feel important when I am being a friend.

1. Be the type of friend you have always wanted to have.

2. Do unto others as they would want you to do unto them.

3. Express appreciation for your friends.

4. Write thank-you notes.

5. Plan a vacation with your friends.

6. Honor your standards and beliefs.

7. Set the tone for your relationships.

8. Join a club or a social group based on your hobbies.

9. Give an anonymous act of service to a friend.

10. Forgive someone and rekindle an old friendship.

I feel important when I am receiving praise.

1. Praise yourself. The more you internalize your emotional fingerprint by praising yourself, the less you will need others to praise you. You will then have the energy to praise others, which, ironically, will give you what you desire, both because they will praise you in return and because in praising them, you will feel as though you *are* praising yourself.

2. Acknowledge your accomplishments by rewarding yourself with something you want.

3. Express gratitude to yourself for all you do.

4. Praise five people a day.

5. Praise a complete stranger in a checkout line.

6. Praise those who are closest to you.

7. Send a thank-you note to someone.

8. Pamper yourself. You know what you need.

9. Take yourself on a date.

10. Spend time with others who need your love: volunteer, visit lonely family members, or share your love with friends and neighbors.

Group 4
I feel important when I am secure.

1. Educate yourself to increase your usefulness.
2. Save 10 percent of the money you make.
3. Be the type of friend you would want to have.
4. Forgive anyone who has wronged you. Emotional security is the best security.
5. Read or study financial or relationship books.
6. Express gratitude for the security you do have.
7. Give service to someone who is not secure.
8. Clearly define what security means to you and make a plan to achieve it.
9. Plan for the future: financially, emotionally, physically, mentally, and spiritually.
10. Let go of old beliefs and habits that make you feel insecure by focusing your energy on creating new and positive habits that make you feel secure.

I feel important when I am being creative.

1. Find a new creative hobby.
2. Take a class at a local college.
3. Learn something new.
4. Study the lives of creative people.
5. Play, play, play creatively.
6. Take time to create.
7. Designate a room for your creativity.
8. Listen to music.
9. Teach others how to be creative.
10. Make a scrapbook, sing, paint, sculpt, plant something, or write.

I feel important when I am healthy.

1. Exercise.
2. Eat right.

3. Learn about healthy food choices.

4. Teach others how to eat in a healthy way.

5. Schedule time to be healthy, whether that means getting sleep, exercise, good food, relaxation, or care from others.

6. Pamper yourself at a spa, a retreat, or a clinic.

7. Hire a personal trainer.

8. Lose undesired weight.

9. Try a new exercise, such as yoga, dance, or cycling.

10. Join a gym and go regularly.

I feel important when I am connected to family.

1. Write a letter to a loved one.

2. Give an anonymous act of service to a family member.

3. Keep a journal about your family.

4. Study your genealogy.

5. Collect family stories.

6. Call family members and let them know you are thinking of them.

7. Read a book on relationships.

8. Forgive someone in your family.

9. Express gratitude for your family.

10. Designate time to focus on reconnecting.

I feel important when I am receiving recognition.

1. Find ways to recognize yourself. When you start to recognize what you do well in your life, you won't need the recognition of others.

2. Keep a journal of things you do well.

3. Every day, list five things you like about yourself.

4. Treat yourself to a little something when you achieve a goal.

5. Keep a running list of your accomplishments.

6. Create a shrine of your successes in your home or your office.
7. Anonymously send thank-you letters to others, recognizing them for what they do.
8. Read self-help books.
9. Renew an old hobby you enjoyed as a child.
10. Focus on things you can control and achieve. Let everything else go.

Group 5
I feel important when I am solving problems.

1. Let go of trying to solve other people's problems.
2. Start a new hobby to give yourself some new problems to solve.
3. Take something apart and put it back together.
4. Master jigsaw puzzles, crosswords, Sudoku, word searches, and other types of mind games.
5. Build something from scratch.
6. Put together a model.
7. Submit your ideas to politicians or educators.
8. Teach someone how to solve problems or fix things.
9. Patch up any old relationships that are suffering.
10. Read books about how things work.

I feel important when I am achieving my life's purpose.

1. Set a standard you are going to live by.
2. Hire a coach to help you achieve your desired results.
3. Clarify your purpose.
4. Surround yourself with people who support your purpose.
5. Support the life purposes of others.
6. Keep a journal of your triumphs.
7. Explore the lives of others who have accomplished their purposes.

8. Be a mentor.

9. Express gratitude for your challenges, because they are part of who you are.

10. Invite people to share in your purpose.

I feel important when I am connected to nature.

1. Participate in an environmental group or cause.

2. Volunteer for something that allows you to feel connected to nature.

3. Hike, ride a bike, go camping, or stroll along the beach.

4. Tend a garden, plant a tree, or pick up trash.

5. Designate time to be in nature.

6. Watch a sunset or a sunrise or walk in the rain.

7. Start your own environmental movement.

8. Plan or sign up for an outdoor activity or sport.

9. Teach the younger generation about nature.

10. Learn how the earth works.

I feel important when I am in a position of influence.

1. Master yourself: your thoughts, your actions, and your impulses.

2. Study the lives of past great leaders.

3. Volunteer, be a mentor, or somehow serve others.

4. Be an active member of your community.

5. Start a company or help someone build theirs.

6. Be a voice for change. Stand up and stand out.

7. Help people to get what they want, and you will get what you want.

8. Feed your mind with inspirational and positive information.

9. Write a book.

10. Lift people up and never tear anyone down.

I feel important when I am validated.

1. Validate yourself to eliminate the desire to have others validate you. In return, you will have more energy to validate others.
2. Validate who you are by accepting and honoring what you do.
3. Validate your purpose on earth.
4. Validate your past and celebrate what you have overcome by listing your accomplishments.
5. Keep a list of the positive things you do throughout the day.
6. Recognize how others differ from you and validate their opinions.
7. Validate people you appreciate by sending cards, notes, text messages, or e-mails.
8. Treat yourself to a little something after achieving a goal.
9. Pray or meditate.
10. Give yourself permission to dream.

Group 6
I feel important when I am reaching my goals.

1. Set small, attainable goals.
2. Reward yourself for reaching your goals with mini celebrations.
3. List it to live it. Write your goals out and post them somewhere you can see them every day.
4. When you are involved in a project, focus on the result.
5. Plan each day, week, and month to attain your desired goal.
6. Sacrifice something small for something greater.
7. Have an accountability partner, that is, someone who holds you accountable to your goals.

8. Make adjustments along the way to help you attain your goals.
9. Let go of goals not achieved. Your past is not your future.
10. Designate time each day or week to work on achieving your goals.

I feel important when I am performing.

1. Teach classes in your chosen field.
2. Join a theater group.
3. Set up speaking engagements.
4. Volunteer in your field.
5. Hire a coach to increase your abilities.
6. Study the top performers in your industry.
7. Practice your skills in front of a mirror.
8. Videotape or digitally record your performances for critiquing.
9. Create a group to practice with.
10. Perform at charity events, hospitals, or shelters.

I feel important when I am learning.

1. Teach. The best form of learning comes from teaching.
2. Pick a new topic to study.
3. Keep a journal of what you have learned.
4. Learn to play a musical instrument.
5. Get a library card and use it.
6. Teach someone to read.
7. Volunteer at a school.
8. Learn to juggle, use a yo-yo, or do magic tricks.
9. Create or join a book club.
10. Travel.

I feel important when I am being a good parent.

1. Take a parenting class.

2. It's all about time. Spend time with your kids.
3. Accept your children for who they are.
4. Be consistent with your discipline.
5. Be your child's greatest advocate.
6. Praise your children's success.
7. Be gentle with your judgments.
8. Remember that it's usually just a phase.
9. Express gratitude for the ups and downs.
10. Leave notes of love for your kids around the house.

I feel important when I am needed.

1. Ironically, the more you give of yourself to others, expecting nothing in return, the more you will feel needed.
2. Volunteer, either publicly or through anonymous service.
3. Lift someone's burdens.
4. Spontaneously help a stranger.
5. Let others know how much you appreciate them.
6. Forgive an old grudge.
7. Meditate or pray and tap into your true identity.
8. Treat yourself to a little pampering.
9. Express gratitude for what you have accomplished in your life.
10. Listen to someone else's problems.

Group 7

I feel important when I am winning.

1. Focus on winning only in your own life. Don't compare yourself to others.
2. Set personal goals that you can achieve so that you feel victorious.
3. Challenge yourself.
4. Take on something new.

5. Create time to win in your life.
6. Organize your life so more things are played like a game.
7. Play more.
8. Study the lives of winners.
9. Raise your standards.
10. Master the things that hold you back.

I feel important when I am experiencing life.

1. Take a trip.
2. Eat something new.
3. Volunteer.
4. Learn something you have always wanted to learn.
5. Challenge yourself.
6. Start a new hobby.
7. Read books, magazines, or literature about how to experience life more fully.
8. Turn off your cell phone, the TV, your computer, or any other personal "time waster" for one day each week.
9. Laugh, smile, hug, and kiss more.
10. Create as much time to play as you can.

I feel important when I am honoring my standards.

1. Define your standards so there is no question of whether you are honoring them.
2. Live with integrity.
3. Be honest.
4. Read about other people who lived by their standards.
5. Forgive yourself and others for violating your standards.
6. Be moral in your thoughts and actions.
7. Be strong in social settings and do not bend to peer pressure.

8. Take an ethics class at a local university.
9. Respect and honor other people's standards.
10. Express gratitude for your standards.

I feel important when I am serving.

1. Volunteer.
2. Give blood.
3. Perform an anonymous act of service.
4. Send thank-you notes to those who have helped you.
5. Be a good listener.
6. Support someone's dream.
7. Offer a shoulder to cry on.
8. Have charity toward all.
9. Help the downtrodden.
10. Recognize people for their efforts.

I feel important when I am accepted.

1. Accept yourself, and you will not need the acceptance of others. You are the only person who can truly accept yourself wholeheartedly.
2. List ten things you do well.
3. Express gratitude for your life, actions, and decisions.
4. Keep a journal of your small victories.
5. Accept others.
6. Validate what you do and who you are.
7. Create and use affirmations.
8. Pray or meditate.
9. Create a shrine of success in your home or office.
10. Reach out to someone who needs help.

PART III

Maximize Your Emotional Fingerprint

7

Clear Your Path

For God has not given us the Spirit of fear; but of power, and of love, and of a sound mind.
—2 Timothy 1:7

Mary Louise Zeller, a dear friend of mine, had some significant obstacles on her path. She saw her eighteen-month-old son fall from a two-story window, and after that trauma she was emotionally paralyzed. Because of her depression she withdrew into a sedentary lifestyle and put on unwanted pounds. Worse, she hovered over her son out of fear, trying to protect him from all of the dangers in the outside world.

Eventually her son fully recovered, but Mary Louise's recovery took longer. Here she tells her story:

> I was depressed. I cried a lot. I could be driving down the road and I'd start crying. The baby helped pull me together. I had to take care of him.
>
> One Sunday morning I was reading the newspaper, and I saw an ad for tae kwon do, and it said, "To improve focus and concentration," of which I had none. It said, "To strengthen self-confidence," of which I had none. I mean,

if you can't keep your own child safe, how good a mother are you? My self-confidence was shattered. I was way overweight and out of shape, and it said, "Get fit." I thought that sounded more fun than running, weight lifting, or aerobics. So I answered the advertisement. I was just going in to check it out, but Master Kim in Vallejo, California, handed me a uniform and said, "Here. Put this on."

There's something about the way a master says, "Here. Put this on." You go, "Oh, okay. I wasn't gonna do that, but okay." He taught me a lesson. He said, "Come back tomorrow." So I did, and I noticed that I felt more alive, and the more active I got, physically, the more settled my mind got and the more settled my emotions got.

The first two weeks, my muscles were so sore, I slept in the bathtub. Really. It was the only place I could sleep. I had to bounce down the stairs on my bottom and crawl up them. I don't know how I kept going, but it gave me a feeling of being alive again. It gave me hope. It did give me self-confidence. The ad was true.

People told me I was too old. I started when I was forty-four. Then came the first time Master Kim said, "I want you to come to a competition." I thought he meant for me to do the mommy things: cheerlead, drive, and make sandwiches. He said, "Oh, no. You will compete."

I went, and I was terrified. I couldn't even get a deep breath, and I just did it anyway. After it was over, I was like, "Wow!" It was like being in high school again, getting on the bus, going to the basketball game. I lost every match I fought for two years. You'd think you would just get discouraged and quit, but I finally went out there, instead of holding back and trying to stay safe—this is full-contact tae kwon do; we wear protective gear in the Olympic style, but it is full contact, so I was trying to be safe.

Well, you can't win trying to be safe. You can be safe trying to be safe, but you can't win. So I just got out there, and I went, "I'm not losing one more time. I'm gonna win this match." That poor opponent of mine, I went after her like a banshee. She was like, "Oh my gosh. Somebody drag this grandmother off of me."

As Mary Louise cleared her path of fear, self-doubt, and worry, she no longer settled for getting beaten. She gained more confidence, and her vision of what was possible expanded. Her story continues:

Somewhere along the line I said, "I want to go to the Olympics." I'm sure that God has a sense of humor now, because to give me the desire to go to the Olympics when I'm fifty-five years old, that's a sense of humor. Everybody thought I was ridiculous, but you know what? I gave 'em a run for their money. In the South they say, "It's better to shoot for the moon and hit the fence than to shoot for the fence and hit the ground." So I shot for the moon. I was fourth in the eighteen-and-over division in full-contact fighting, which requires speed, strength, stamina, endurance, and amazing quickness.

You really have to have a big dream to be alive. Power and passion in life—live in that domain. The power of internalizing your emotional fingerprint is to actually be at the source of power. When I'm making a difference, I'm happy. I'd like to inspire you: Look, you don't have to expect to be drooling in an old folks' home when you get older. When I'm eighty, I'm gonna be on the mat, in some form or fashion—on some mat. I'm gonna be on the mat, playing the game.

The one thing I would like to leave you with is something that your coach will tell you: "Leave it on the mat." When you go out to give it all, and you know you gave it all, it is so rich. Leave it on the mat. So when you think you don't have anything left to give, you've got everything to give. Leave it on the mat. Leave it all. Don't leave this life without leaving it all. Just give it.

Mary Louise is still competing at the age of sixty-seven. She competes in the eighteen-and-older division in tae kwon do. Yes, you read that correctly. She competes with people nearly fifty years younger rather than competing with her peers in the sixty-and-older division.

Even though she was terrified for two years and lost every match, she managed to clear her path of fear and worry, which enabled her to take her first championship. Today, she is a sixth-degree black belt and a master instructor in Olympic sport tae kwon do. She is a seventeen-time U.S. National Gold Medalist and an eight-time International Gold Medalist. On invitation, she trained with the 2000 U.S. Olympic team at the U.S. Olympic Training Center in Colorado Springs, Colorado.

In 2004 Mary Louise was inducted into the U.S. Martial Arts Hall of Fame and was acknowledged as the International Female Competitor of the Year. At the Korean Open in 2004, she was also awarded the prestigious Hwarang Warrior Award for Female Competitor of the Year. Mary Louise is the current U.S. National Gold Medalist in technique and forms in the eighteen and older division. She is still dreaming about new goals—and pursuing them. She no longer lets fear, self-doubt, and worry keep her from maximizing her emotional fingerprint. She has learned how to clear her path.

Maximizing Your Emotional Fingerprint

We've seen how becoming aware of your emotional fingerprint allows you to master your emotional highs and lows and to make conscious, effective decisions about your life. We've seen how internalizing your emotional fingerprint enables you to develop enormous emotional reserves, giving you the resilience to weather life's obstacles and to take back power over your life. The third step on the path to owning your life is to maximize your emotional fingerprint: to pursue the dreams and goals that allow you to reach your highest potential, to achieve everything you are capable of, and to fully express every aspect of your emotional fingerprint in the ways that will be the most satisfying to you.

What could possibly keep you from doing this? In my experience as a coach, there are three ways you might have problems:

1. You run into fear, worry, and anxiety, which blocks your path.
2. You become caught up in unrealistic expectations, which are generally external, rather than focusing on personal standards, which are by definition internal.
3. You do not sharpen your resolve and focus on what matters most to you.

In these final chapters, we'll look at each of these obstacles. If I were forced to focus on only one, however, it would have to be the subject of this chapter: fear. This is the obstacle that blocks the vast majority of the people I coach, and it is only when they clear their paths of fear that they begin to take enormous strides toward making their dreams come true. If you are going to maximize your emotional fingerprint, you need to learn how to clear your path of fear.

Our first step, as usual, is understanding. What is fear and why is it so powerful? Let's take a closer look.

Fear Is Always in the Future

Let's say you're hiking in the hills and as the trail winds past a tree, you suddenly see a huge rattlesnake in the middle of the trail. What would you be afraid it would do? If you are like most people, you would be afraid that the snake would bite you. Now let's say you take a step back and it does bite you, right in the leg.

What are you afraid is going to happen? Again, if you are like most people, you would be afraid that the venom will poison you and you will die. Note that your dominant emotion is not about something in the present. You don't feel resentment that the snake has interrupted your thoughts or frustration with the pain in your leg. You fear something that might happen in the future: that the snakebite means you are going to die.

I have purposely chosen an example in which the fear is of physical death rather than financial failure, personal humiliation, or romantic frustration. Although pretty much any obstacle in life can at least potentially be overcome, death puts an end to all of our efforts. Fear of death—the need to maintain our safety and to engage in self-preservation—trumps every other kind of fear.

I have also chosen an example in which the fear is entirely realistic. A rattling, hissing snake in your path might well strike. A rattlesnake bite will almost certainly kill you. In this case, your fear is entirely justified.

Even in this case, though, your fear is not responding to what *is* happening but to what you perceive is *going* to happen. You are afraid in the present because of something that you believe—in this case, correctly—will probably happen in the future.

The Two Types of Fear

All fear concerns something that we believe will or might happen in the future, and this fear may be divided into two types. One type is crucial to our survival. The other has helpful aspects, alerting us to take some aspects of our situation into account, but by and large, the second type is perhaps the most common obstacle to maximizing the emotional fingerprint.

The first type of fear is born of self-preservation. It concerns actual, immediate threats to our physical safety and that of the people we love. An attacker, a traffic accident, a serious illness, a major storm, and a fire are actual, immediate threats that are quite different from, for instance, the prospect of being laid off or even of being destitute and having to beg for food.

Clearly, self-preservation fear serves a very useful purpose. It warns us of genuine danger and helps us to avoid taking risks that might maim, cripple, or kill us. Self-preservation fear teaches us to be cautious around rattlesnakes, heavy traffic, hot stoves, and violent people. It encourages us to take extra water when we travel across the desert and reminds us to fasten our seat belts when we drive. It makes us teach our kids to look both ways before crossing the street and inspires us to keep our smoke alarms supplied with fresh batteries. Genuine self-preservation is based on realistic concerns about dangers that could threaten our physical safety and that of the people we love.

The other type of fear, the kind that blocks our paths and prevents us from maximizing our emotional fingerprints, I describe with the acronym FEAR, for "false evidence appearing real." Whereas fear of the rattlesnake or the auto accident is based on *truth*, or authentic evidence—there really is a danger out there, and we need to take immediate, physical action to defend ourselves—this other type of fear is *false*. It is not giving us any useful information about the world. It is false evidence appearing real.

This kind of fear is false, because it is based on the faulty premise that we can actually know the future. We can't, of course. We rightly fear anything that threatens our physical survival because death is certain to end our future on this planet. Any other kind of threat, though, has an uncertain outcome. Even if we have reason to believe that the initial outcome of a threat will be dire—public shame, bankruptcy, jail, or the loss of a loved one—we have no idea what the *ultimate* outcome will be. None. We simply cannot know what the future will bring, which is why our fears of it are simply wasted energy. Mark Twain once said, "I've experienced many terrible things in my life, a few of which actually happened." William Shakespeare expressed the same thought even more eloquently: "Cowards die many times before their deaths."

The sad thing is that this type of fear does *not* lead to self-preservation and is often actually harmful. Decades of research have proved the ill effects of stress, anxiety, fear, and constant worrying. There is no doubt that they harm the body, the mind, and the soul. Have you ever been so stressed out and worried that you couldn't sleep? Were you ever so afraid to make a decision that you just didn't make one at all? Have you ever been so anxious that your heart pounded, your blood pressure rose, and you felt sick to your stomach? Mystery writer Arthur Somers Roche eloquently explained, "Anxiety is a thin stream of fear trickling through the mind. If encouraged, it cuts a channel into which all other thoughts are drained."

The Power of Fear

Why is fear so powerful? Why does it so often block us from maximizing our emotional fingerprints?

To find the answer, we have to take a look at how our bodies are wired. In the brain there are two one-inch almond-shaped clusters that make up what is called the *amygdala*. This structure, sometimes called the "emotional brain," is responsible for cuing us to respond instantly in case of an immediate, physical threat. In fact, the amygdala's message reaches the nervous system even before the "thinking brain"—the cerebral cortex—has a chance to weigh in. In the example of encountering a snake, the amygdala will instruct our bodies to jump out of the way even before the cerebral cortex has had the chance to identify the snake as a harmless garter snake or an even more harmless tree branch.

The fast-acting amygdala gets priority access in our brains because physical survival is our number one priority. "Act first and ask questions later" may be an excellent motto if we're jumping out of the way of a rattlesnake or using the fear-based adrenaline rush to outrun a charging elephant. If we read about a dip in the stock market, get a "we have to talk" text from a boyfriend or girlfriend, or receive a call from an angry relative, we might still have a similar panic response. Fears about the economy, our relationships, or our personal lives might lead us to picture bankruptcy, homelessness, divorce, or abandonment, creating the same intensity and urgency we would feel if we actually were encountering the poisonous snake or the charging elephant.

The amygdala sparks the fight-or-flight response, in which we either fight back in a situation or run away from it. The amygdala revs up the heart, the lungs, the blood flow, and the muscles, preparing us for a life-or-death physical effort. With an emotional problem or a possible future danger, a physical response in the present won't help, yet our repertoire is extremely limited here: either the amygdala reacts or it doesn't. It can't distinguish a threat to our survival (such as a snake) from a threat to our emotions (such as an announced layoff at work) from an imagined threat (such as fearing that we might encounter a snake on next week's camping trip or worrying that an economic downturn might lead to layoffs). In all three cases—physical, emotional, and imagined—the physical experience of fear is virtually identical. Dr. Maxwell Maltz, said, "Experimental and clinical psychologists have proven beyond a shadow of a doubt that the human nervous system cannot tell the difference between an actual experience and an experience imagined vividly and in detail."

The stress response to fear, originally discovered by Harvard physiologist Walter Cannon, is hardwired into our brains and represents a genetic wisdom designed to protect us from bodily harm. When it is stimulated, this response signals an area of the brain called the hypothalamus, which initiates a sequence of nerve cell firings and chemical releases that prepare the body for running or fighting—even when that is not an appropriate reaction to the perceived threat.

Thus, for many of us, toxic stress hormones flow into our bodies on a daily basis in response to events that pose no real threat to our physical survival. Many of today's stresses in the business and personal realm trigger the full activation of the fight-or-flight response, creating an ongoing condition in us of "permanent warfare." What is worse, the body can't shut down the response instantaneously, even when we realize that the threat isn't real. Once the stress chemicals have been released into the blood, they must be cleared by enzymes and proteins—but this takes time. While these chemical messengers circulate and our systems remain hyped up, we can become aggressive, hypervigilant, and, at times, overreactive. Instead of saving our responses for fear, we mobilize them for FEAR.

Each individual has a personal FEAR. It may be a fear of dating or of intimacy, of a boss, of being unemployed, of asking for a promotion, or of a thousand other things. Even though you know you won't die from whatever it is that you are afraid of, emotionally you feel the FEAR as though death itself threatened your body. Feeling intense fear or anxiety is uncomfortable and, in large doses, bad for your health, but that's not even the worst part. The worst part is that your FEAR keeps you from maximizing your emotional fingerprint. Because you're afraid to pursue your dreams, to choose the actions that will help you to validate your aspects of importance, you hold back, shortchanging yourself and your loved ones by not becoming all you might have been. FEAR is the culprit—false evidence appearing real. The problem is that the false evidence just *seems* so real.

EXERCISE

What FEAR Is Blocking Your Path?

Take a moment to consider how fears, worry, and anxiety might be blocking your path and preventing you from maximizing your emotional fingerprint. Complete the following sentences:

In My Personal Life

1. I would love to _____ if I weren't afraid of
    _____.

2. I have always wished I could _____,
    but I didn't because _____.

3. Something I frequently worry about is _____.

4. Something I would never dare to do is _____.

5. Something that holds me back from maximizing my emotional
    fingerprint is _____.

In My Relationships

6. I would love to _____ if I weren't afraid of
    _____.

7. I have always wished I could _____,
    but I didn't because _____.

8. Something I frequently worry about is _____.

9. Something I would never dare to do is _____.

10. Something that holds me back from maximizing my emotional fingerprint is _____.

In My Work Life

11. I would love to _____ if I weren't afraid of

_____.

12. I have always wished I could _____,
    but I didn't because _____

_____.

13. Something I frequently worry about is _____.

14. Something I would never dare to do is _____.

15. Something that holds me back from maximizing my emotional fingerprint is _____.

Look at your responses to the previous questions and then answer the following questions:

1. What might be the benefits to you if you could overcome your fears in your personal life?

_____

_____

2. What might be the benefits to you if you could overcome your fears in your relationships?

_____

_____

3. What might be the benefits to you if you could overcome your fears in your work life?

_____

_____

Overcome Fear by Living in the Present

Whether we are talking about self-preservation or FEAR, one thing is true: you cannot feel fear when you are fully present in the moment. You may feel the effects of the amygdala shooting sparks to your nervous system, causing your heart to race and creating the illusion that oxygen is hard to come by, and you may become acutely aware of your surroundings, but you can learn to interpret this feeling as heightened awareness or hyperalertness rather than as dread, anxiety, or worry. Focusing on the present allows you to convert this heightened state into a positive experience or at least a helpful one, much as actors do before a live performance or as athletes do before a big game.

You can also ask yourself whether this state of hyperalertness is giving you useful information that will help you to preserve your life or is just false information appearing real. Look at the following lists. Can you see the difference between fear that's based on authentic evidence and fear that's based on false evidence?

Authentic Evidence

I'm driving on an icy road. I might have an accident.

My child is learning to walk. She might run into traffic.

I am going hiking, and it has started to snow. I might get lost or stuck.

Helpful Responses

I'll drive extra carefully and be hyperalert.

I'll hold her hand when we are near a street.

I'll turn back to avoid getting caught in a blizzard.

False Evidence

I am leaving for a trip tomorrow. What if I don't have the right clothes? What if I miss my plane?

My boss looked at me in a funny way today. What if he's mad at me?

My boyfriend didn't call me back. What if he's losing interest or maybe even has found someone else?

Unhelpful Responses

I'll worry a lot about what to pack and wake up throughout the night, because I'll be afraid that the alarm won't go off.

I'll worry about not getting my end-of-year bonus and maybe even about getting fired.

I'll worry about him leaving me. I'll imagine how hard it will be to find another boyfriend and remember how awful it is to be single.

Any of the fears in the second list's right-hand column may certainly be warranted. You might pack the wrong things or miss the plane. You might lose a bonus or get fired. Your relationship may be in trouble, and perhaps you will be single again soon.

The problem is that none of the anxiety and worry is leading you to helpful responses. Once you have finished packing and set your alarm, your worries are not helping you to prepare any better. If you have forgotten something, worrying won't help you to remember it. If your alarm clock is broken, worrying won't fix it. Unless you think that you really might need to repack your suitcase or arrange for another way to wake up, your fears aren't helping you—they're just making you miserable.

Likewise, your initial worry about your job or your relationship might prompt some kind of useful action, such as talking to your boss or your boyfriend to find out more about how he feels. Once you've decided on an action, fear won't help you to improve that decision. Worry doesn't help you to plan for a future in which you are unemployed, nor does it inspire new ideas about how to meet your next boyfriend, especially when you don't even know whether you *will* be unemployed or single. FEAR, worry, and anxiety *appear* to be giving you good information: "Look, look, danger is coming! Get out of the way!" In fact, these emotions are not alerting you to any actual danger. They're simply undermining your confidence.

Maybe we hold on to our FEAR because we like to believe that we can see into the future—even if what we see is negative. Perhaps imagining the worst possible outcome gives us the illusion of control, as though we have somehow decided our own fates. Maybe believing that we know what's going to happen—even if it's a depressing, miserable outcome—feels better than accepting that we *don't* know what's going to happen.

I'm not sure why it's so tempting to listen to our fears, because however much we might like to know what the future holds, none of us does. In some cases, your fear might be cuing you to an actual possibility: perhaps that funny look *does* mean that your boss is mad at you—or maybe he was simply thinking of something else.

Your fear goes past any possible reality into a terrible future: angry boss equals job loss equals destitution and misery. That future is something you simply made up. Even supposing that your boss *is* mad, you might not lose your job. Perhaps you will lose your job and decide to start your own business, or you might walk out of your office and then five minutes later get the best job offer of your life. You really don't know what the future holds, no matter how loudly your fear insists that you do.

Likewise, your boyfriend's missed call *might* be a terrible warning signal, indicating that he is ready to leave you—or it might only mean that he was busy and couldn't pick up the phone. FEAR is a potential event that may or may not come true. In the worst-case scenario, let's suppose that it does come true and you find yourself single. You could find out that you love being single again, in ways you never expected. What if you are suddenly deluged with invitations from interesting, exciting men that you never could have accepted if you were still committed to your boyfriend? What if the day after your boyfriend leaves you, you meet a new man who turns out to be the love of your life?

In either case—losing your job or your boyfriend—your worst fear might come true, yet everything could turn out better than before. You thought you knew the future, and you weren't completely wrong—but in the end, you weren't right, either. None of us knows what the future holds—but our fears are *false evidence* telling us that we do.

There is a wonderful Buddhist parable that expresses this idea perfectly. A farmer once owned a beautiful stallion, and his neighbors all envied him. When they congratulated him on his good fortune, however, the farmer simply said, "Perhaps."

Then the horse ran away. The neighbors all commiserated, saying, "What terrible luck!" The farmer simply said, "Perhaps."

Then the horse came back, leading a wild mare and a little colt. Now, instead of one horse, the farmer had three. The neighbors said, "What good fortune!" and the farmer again said, "Perhaps."

Then the farmer's son tried to train the young colt but was crippled when the wild horse threw him. However, when war was declared and all of the young men in the village were conscripted, only the farmer's crippled son was exempted. The neighbors called the accident bad news and the exemption good news, but the farmer understood that we're never in control of the ultimate outcome of any action, plan, or situation. With the future always out of reach, unknowable and uncontrollable, fear is always a waste of time. "Perhaps" was the farmer's only response, avoiding the trap of FEAR.

Fear and Your Emotional Fingerprint

Everyone has false fears that block his or her path. In fact, fears are customized to an individual's emotional fingerprint. Here is the definition of FEAR as it applies to your emotional fingerprint: false evidence appearing real is the anticipation of a potential circumstance in which your aspects of importance will be disrespected.

My client Michael had a hard time with this concept. He insisted that his fears were reasonable and that he was responding intelligently and accurately to potential dangers. Michael worried constantly about being laid off from his job as a middle manager in marketing. He worried that his beloved wife, who traveled frequently on business, might find someone at work with whom she might have an affair, perhaps even leaving him as a result. He worried that his two children, whom he adored, would do poorly in school and not get into college, therefore facing a dire and unhappy future. His life was eaten up by worries that he insisted were rational concerns about real dangers threatening him and his family.

As someone who once had to move into my parents' basement with a wife and an infant son after losing everything financially, I was sympathetic. I understood that bad things can and do happen to everyone, and that no matter how strong, brave, or clear thinking we are, we can't always prevent them. My research into the lives of successful people had also shown me that many of them suffered from and struggled against unbelievable odds: failed businesses, devastating accidents, the loss of a loved one. People like Harriet

Tubman, Viktor Frankl, and Nelson Mandela even faced enslavement, imprisonment, and possible death as the entire resources of an oppressive society were turned against them.

Yet I could also see that Michael's fears were not protecting him from possible dangers. His fears about losing his job did not inspire him to work more effectively or to get along better with his employer and his colleagues. His fears about losing his marriage did not help him to become a more loving husband. His fears for his children did not make him a more effective father.

If anything, Michael's fears had the opposite effect, making him less safe and certainly less happy. At work, fear kept Michael from making the kinds of strong, clear, confident decisions that might have made his job more secure or helped him to pursue opportunities for better positions elsewhere. Fears in his family relationships caused him to push away his wife and try to control his children, which made his family life worse and kept Michael from enjoying time with his loved ones.

All of the things Michael worried about would indeed have caused him pain *if* they had happened. By worrying about them *before* they happened, Michael was spoiling his own life. Moreover, even if the worst *had* happened, Michael had no way of knowing what might happen next. Sometimes the most painful tragedies lead to a richer, fuller, more joyous life.

In my view, Michael's fears were keeping him from maximizing his emotional fingerprint, so one day I asked him to express his fears to me in those terms. "I think every one of your fears is related to your emotional fingerprint being disrespected," I told him. "Let's look at each aspect of your emotional fingerprint and see how your fears relate."

Michael's Emotional Fingerprint
1. Being trusted
2. Providing
3. Working
4. Feeling connected to family
5. Solving problems

6. Being a good parent
7. Being accepted

Here is what Michael wrote about his emotional fingerprint and his primary fears:

1. Losing my job. All seven aspects of my emotional fingerprint are disrespected:
   - Being trusted. My employer can't trust me to do a good job. My family can't trust me to take care of them. I can't trust myself to succeed.
   - Providing. I won't be able to provide for my family.
   - Working. I won't be working—losing my job means I can't work.
   - Feeling connected to family. I can't face my family if I lose my job. I will have to avoid everyone until I find another one, because I will feel so ashamed and everyone will look down on me.
   - Solving problems. Losing my job means that I couldn't solve my problems. I am a failure as a problem solver, because otherwise I could have solved the problem of how to keep my job!
   - Being a good parent. What kind of father doesn't keep his job so he can provide his children with the things they need? What kind of example am I setting for my kids if I can't keep my job?
   - Being accepted. Losing my job means that my employer did not accept me. Maybe no employer will ever accept me! My children, wife, relatives, and neighbors will not accept me, because a man without a job is a real failure.
2. Losing my wife. Five aspects of importance are disrespected:
   - Being trusted. My wife would not trust me to be the man she wants. I would not trust myself to be a good husband who can hold on to his wife.
   - Providing. How can I provide for my wife if she leaves me? If she leaves me, it was because I wasn't a good

provider. I didn't provide her with enough love, security, or financial support.

- Feeling connected to family. If my wife leaves me, I will have lost my family. I won't be happy at gatherings of my own family, either. Everyone will see what a failure I am as a husband and will look down on me. I will feel lonely as a divorced man when I look at my married parents and siblings, so I won't enjoy family get-togethers or visits.

- Solving problems. If my wife leaves me, that means I couldn't solve the problem of how to make her happy. I won't be able to solve the problem of finding someone else to love who will love me back. I won't be able to solve the problem of making that potential second wife happy, either!

- Being accepted. If my wife leaves me, she did not accept me. If I can't make her happy, I can't accept myself. I will be a failure who doesn't deserve to be accepted.

3. Something bad happening to my children. Six aspects are disrespected:

    - Being trusted. My children don't trust me to take care of them. My wife wouldn't trust me to take care of my kids. How can I trust myself to take care of my kids? Bad things can happen to them, and I can't trust myself to protect them!

    - Providing. What if I can't give my kids everything they need to be safe and happy and have a good future?

    - Feeling connected to family. Family is the most important thing in the world. If I fail my kids, I won't have a family. I will let my family down—my wife and my kids as well as all of my relatives.

    - Solving problems. The most important problem in my life is how to protect my kids. Every time something bad happens to them and every time they are unhappy, I have failed to solve their problems.

    - Being a good parent. If anything bad happens to my kids, that means I was a bad parent.

- Being accepted. I would not accept myself if I could not protect my kids. No one would be able to accept me. No one should accept me, because I will have failed as a father.

After Michael completed this exercise, he was struck by how deeply his fears related to his emotional fingerprint. "What you are really afraid of, every time, is that your aspects of importance will be disrespected," I told him. "So the solution to your fears is to find another way to validate and support your aspects of importance. If you can truly internalize your emotional fingerprint—if you can find an *internal* way to validate each of your aspects of importance—your fears will lose their power."

EXERCISE

How Your Fears Affect Your Emotional Fingerprint

To see how your fears relate to your emotional fingerprint, complete the following chart. You can use major fears, such as losing your job, or minor fears, such as the anxiety that many people feel before taking a trip.

My Fears	Aspects Disrespected If Fears Came True
_____	_____
	_____
_____	_____
	_____
_____	_____
	_____

Internalizing Your Emotional Fingerprint to Overcome Your Fears

I asked Michael to find a way to internally validate every aspect of importance of his emotional fingerprint that was threatened by his fears. I wanted him to see that the way to overcome his fears was not by worrying harder or even by trying to talk himself out of them but by focusing on what he *could* control. I wanted him to see that validating his emotional fingerprint internally was *always* within his power. We can always be happy in the present, because fear is always about the future. If our physical safety or our loved ones' physical safety is threatened *in the present*, then of course we need to take action. In every other circumstance, fear is false evidence appearing real.

Here is how Michael internalized his emotional fingerprint:

1. Losing my job
    *   Being trusted. I trust myself to be a good worker and a good colleague. I trust myself to handle anything that life throws at me. I would give my life for my family, so I trust myself to find a way to take care of them. True, I don't know right now how I would take care of them if I lost my job. But if and when that happens, I trust myself to handle it.
    *   Providing. I will always provide my family with love and emotional support. No one can ever stop me from loving them and doing what I think is best for them.
    *   Working. If I lose my job, I will work hard at finding a new one. I will find projects at home that I can work on while I am unemployed. I might work at starting a new business. I might work at a job for free to convince a new employer to hire me.
    *   Feeling connected to family. I will remain open and loving to my family whether or not I have a job. If they don't respond well to that, I will keep my connection to them alive in my heart.
    *   Solving problems. If I lose my job, I will solve the problem of what to do next. I am a good problem solver, and I will solve that problem, too.
    *   Being a good parent. If I lose my job, I will model for my children how a man meets adversity and doesn't give up, and I will show them how they too can survive and

triumph. When they grow up, they will know that they can face any obstacle, because of how I helped them face this one.

- Being accepted. I accept myself as a good worker and a good man. Losing my job has no effect on my decision to accept myself.

2. Losing my wife

- Being trusted. I trust myself to be a loving husband and a good man. I trust myself to do everything in my power to make my relationship work. If it is not in my power to succeed and I lose my wife's love, I trust myself to handle the situation.

- Providing. I will provide my wife with all my love and emotional support. If she leaves me, I will provide myself with the love and emotional support I need to move on and find someone else to love.

- Feeling connected to family. I will remain open and loving to my family, regardless of what my wife does. I will treasure those connections and find ways to enjoy them, with or without my wife.

- Solving problems. I will solve the problem of how to keep my relationship working well or of how to cope with it falling apart. I accept that no problem solver in the world has complete control over outcomes. I will define *problem solving* as "giving it my best effort" rather than "controlling the outcome."

- Being accepted. I will accept myself no matter what my wife chooses to do.

3. Something bad happening to my kids

- Being trusted. I trust myself to do everything in my power to protect my children. I accept that I don't have complete control over what happens to them.

- Providing. I will provide my children with all my love and emotional support. I can always do that, no matter what else happens.

- Feeling connected to family. I will hold my connection to my family in my heart and remain open to every family member who wishes to connect to me.

- Solving problems. I will solve the problem of how to protect my children or of what to do if they get into trouble. I accept that no problem solver in the world has complete control over outcomes. I will define *problem solving* as "giving it my best effort" rather than "controlling the outcome."

- Being a good parent. I will define a *good parent* as someone who always tries his best to be there for his kids rather than as someone who has the power to protect them. I accept that no parent in the world has complete control over outcomes for his kids.

- Being accepted. I will accept myself no matter what happens to my children.

Michael had been a worrier all his life, and it wasn't easy for him to give up his fears, but by finding internal validation for his emotional fingerprint every time a fear came up, he managed to let fear go. He found it very helpful to remind himself that his fears were giving him false information that he should ignore rather than true information that he should listen to. This understanding allowed him to relax and respond more in the moment instead of constantly defending himself from his fears.

As my friend Mary Louise put it at the beginning of this chapter, "You can't win trying to be safe. You can be safe trying to be safe, but you can't win." When Michael learned this lesson, he became more relaxed and open, at home and at work. His job performance improved enormously, and his relationships with his family became far more satisfying. Michael even began thinking about leaving his current job to take a better one, an option that he had always ignored before because he had been so terrorized by the possibility that he might not be able to keep working and provide for his family. He put aside the false evidence of his fears and pushed away their deceptive message about the future.

His reward was to maximize his emotional fingerprint in every part of his life—and to feel the joy and satisfaction that inevitably followed.

EXERCISE

Identifying Internal Ways to Overcome Your Fears

Look at the fears you identified in the previous exercise and at the aspects of your emotional fingerprint that they tapped into. Identify internal ways to validate each aspect of importance. Then complete the following chart:

My Fears   Internal Ways to Validate Each Aspect

_____   _____

                                    _____

                                    _____

_____   _____

                                    _____

                                    _____

_____   _____

                                    _____

                                    _____

Other Ways to Overcome Your Fears

There are four additional steps you can take to clear your path of fear so that you can go out into the world and maximize your emotional fingerprint:

- Have a dream bigger than your obstacle.
- Live in the now.
- Experiment to prove that your fears aren't real.
- Trade emotion for emotion.

Have a Dream Bigger Than Your Obstacle

Many of my clients are held back by the fear that if they try something difficult—such as starting a business or marketing a new
product—they might fail. I ask them what's so bad about failure,
and they always stare at me in disbelief.

Now, however, we have seen the spectacular failures in our
nation's finance industry—failures that don't seem to have deterred
the people responsible from continuing in the same positions at the
same astronomical salaries. So I can ask my clients why *they* are so
afraid of failure.

"You've got some of the smartest people on the planet, in
charge of finances, and they all failed!" I say. "So what is *your*
excuse for not even trying? Obviously, they screwed up! If they
get to make mistakes, why don't you get to make mistakes? And
they're still moving forward—they're still losing trillions! If they're
not defeated, why are you?"

So many of us are afraid of failing and looking bad, but I tell
my clients that failure is not failure; it is a delay in results, and it is
part of success. You cannot achieve great days without knowing a
few dark nights. It is your ability to pick yourself up when you fall
that will make you successful in your personal life, in relationships,
and in business. Legendary basketball star Michael Jordan said,
"I've missed more than 9,000 shots. I've lost almost 300 games. I've
failed over and over again in my life. And that is why I succeed."

Your failures, setbacks, and hardships do not define who you
are or will become. They are only individual snapshots of individual
situations—isolated experiences in which you thought you failed.
They are not a road map of your life; they are not a compass point-
ing to what you will become. The future is always unwritten.

The bigger the dreams and the more ambitious the goals, the
bigger the obstacles often are. Suppose you want to start your
own business, and your credit card company sends you a letter
informing you that your credit line has been lowered. If you didn't
have the dream of starting your own business, this might merely
be annoying—your family couldn't go out to dinner as often, or

maybe you'd would have to defer buying some new furniture. If you were counting on your credit cards to help you get through the transition from employee to entrepreneur, however, this reduction in your credit line might make the difference between starting your dream now or later—or maybe even not at all. If you didn't have a big dream, the event would just be difficult. Because you have a dream, the event is a massive obstacle.

The solution is to find a dream that is bigger than your obstacle— a dream that truly seems to be the maximization of your emotional fingerprint. When you have a dream that you think can maximize who you are, the passion you feel for your dream can help you to overcome your fears.

The dream that has the most chance of pulling you past your fears is the dream that maximizes your emotional fingerprint. If your dream promises to validate one aspect of importance of your emotional fingerprint, that's terrific, but a dream that validates two or three aspects will be even more magnetic. A dream that validates five, six, or seven of your aspects will probably motivate you to go to the edge, taking whatever risks are necessary. Those who live on the edge have the best view.

If you are looking for a dream that is bigger than its obstacles, I suggest that you ask yourself, "If I could do anything in the world and knew I would not fail, what would I do?" The answer to that question is usually the best way for you to maximize your emotional fingerprint.

Live in the Now

As we have seen, fear is always about the future. So the way to overcome your fear is to live in the now as much as possible.

This isn't always easy, and, in my experience, it takes practice. You can turn to approaches such as yoga, tai chi, martial arts, dance, or meditation to help you live more in the moment, or you can simply keep reminding yourself that you don't know what the future will bring. The past is behind you; the future does not exist; the moment is now.

Some people find that a spiritual or religious perspective is helpful to living in the now. Many religious traditions have parables, proverbs, or sayings that remind us that the future is not in our hands. In addition to the Buddhist parable I quoted earlier, there are several New Testament verses that instruct us not to worry, such as this passage from Matthew 6:25, 34: "Therefore I say unto you, Take no thought for your life, what ye shall eat, or what ye shall drink; nor yet for your body, what ye shall put on. . . . Take therefore no thought for the morrow: for the morrow shall take thought for the things of itself. Sufficient unto the day is the evil thereof."

Jewish tradition likewise has many approaches to overcoming anxiety. "We must not worry," wrote Rabbi Lekhivitz a Polish Hasidic rabbi of the early twentieth century. "Only one worry is permissible: a person should worry because he is worrying."

Another way to transcend fear and focus on the now is to find a spiritual connection through music or art. Gazing at a beautiful painting or listening to your favorite piece of music can allow you to detach from your anxieties and ground yourself in your immediate experience. Time spent in nature, vigorous physical activity, and playing with an animal can all help you to focus on the *now* instead of the "what if." One of my favorite ways to let go of worry is to spend time with my kids, just playing with them and entering their world.

Anything you can do to live in the now is helpful, because it reminds you that ultimately, all you have is every single moment of your life, lived one by one. My family and I were at Disneyland one day, in the line at Autotopia, and I was on my phone, texting and sending e-mails. My brilliant wife turned to me and said, "Why have moments if you can't be in the moment?" I knew what she was saying. Here I was at the "Happiest Place on Earth" with my family, and I was worried about my business, my clients, and my e-mail. If you live in the moment, you will begin to enjoy each moment more. Maximizing your emotional fingerprint can happen only in each moment, as you live it, letting go of fear and opening up to joy.

Experiment to Prove to Yourself That Your Fears Aren't Real

One day, a graduate student rushed into his statistics class late and saw two problems written on the board. Assuming they were homework, he jotted them down and took them home to solve. A few days later he gave them to his professor, apologizing for having taken so long, commenting that they seemed to be a little harder than usual. He asked if the professor even wanted the homework at this late date, and the professor told him to throw it on his desk. The student was reluctant to leave his work—the desk was buried in papers, and he thought the homework might be lost—but he put down the pages and thought no more about it.

About six weeks later, at eight o'clock on a Sunday morning, the student and his wife heard a banging on the door. It was the professor. He came in with the homework and said, "I've just written an introduction to one of your papers. Read it so I can send it out right away for publication." The student had no idea what the professor was talking about.

It turned out that the two problems on the board were famous unsolved problems in statistics, theorems that no one had ever been able to prove. Had the graduate student been to class on time, he would have heard the professor, Jerzy Neyman, explain that the problems had never been solved, so very likely he would have been too afraid to even try and fail.

The student, George Dantzig, had a long and productive career in mathematics after his initial "mistaken" triumph, which took place in 1939. In 1975, he was awarded the National Medal of Science. The incident passed into urban legend and has been repeated in many different versions over the years, as well as providing the basis for an early scene in the movie *Good Will Hunting*, in which a janitor solves a problem that top graduate students had been unable to crack. The story sounds too good to be true, but it *is* true, and it stands as a testament to how much we can accomplish when fear doesn't hold us back.

You may not want to go out and solve major mathematical problems, but you *can* experiment to prove that your fears aren't real. I tell my clients to do it all the time. Break your dream down into the smallest "bite-sized" pieces you can and take the tiniest possible steps toward making it come true. Remember to define your success or failure in *internal* terms—according to what you can control. If you want to write a novel, start with a single page or even just a paragraph. If you want to start a business, choose a domain name for your website. If you want to enter a new relationship, smile at a stranger and see if you can engage him or her in conversation, with no agenda beyond a three-minute chat. Do something—anything—to maximize your emotional fingerprint, then do a bit more, and then a bit more. Before you know it, you'll have cleared your path of fear.

Remember that fear lives in the future, but we live in the present. Fear says, "You won't be able to do it." The present says, "Look, I'm doing it! In fact, I just did something, and now I'm doing something more."

Trade Emotion for Emotion

The airplane door clicked shut as I settled into my seat. I was on my way to present my work to a crowd at a sold-out event. As I sat in my seat counting my blessings and reflecting on my success, I received a call from a panicked client. Kendall's breathing raced as he described how a certain person was destroying his business and he couldn't handle it anymore. He mentioned all of the negative thoughts he had toward this individual and told me that he was afraid he was going to act on his impulses, losing his temper and undoing all of his efforts with one foolish act.

Kendall was a territory manager of a multimillion-dollar real estate coaching company. I had been consulting him for three months, and I considered him an exemplary learner. We had increased his personal income of twenty to thirty thousand dollars a month to more than a hundred thousand dollars a month. His family and his personal life were wonderful as well. He had used the tools and techniques that I teach and was getting fabulous results—until that call.

"Woody," he said, "I understand everything you've told me, and I've gone through my workbook and journals, but nothing is working. What do I do?"

I was so shocked that I didn't know what to say, especially since the pilot had just come on the overhead speaker and told us to turn off all electronic devices. I didn't want to leave Kendall in this emotional state as I took my cross-country flight, but I knew I had to get off the phone. I promised to call him the second the plane landed, and I put the phone away.

Where were all of those feelings of success and gratitude I had experienced just a few minutes ago? They all seemed to have flown right out the window as we ascended to thirty thousand feet. All I could think was that I'd taught Kendall everything I knew, and it wasn't working. I had coached thousands of people throughout the years, and no one had ever had this reaction. What was I missing?

I took a deep breath and shifted my focus to a calm confidence within me and its ability to produce results. I said a little silent prayer and started to search my mind for the answer. Then it occurred to me: emotion for emotion.

Kendall logically understood that there was no reason for fear. He comprehended the principles behind internalizing his emotional fingerprint, but he hadn't yet implemented this knowledge in his life on an emotional level.

In chapter 6 we saw how to create reassociations, new ways of thinking about actions, people, and places. You will recall, for example, that I reassociated the fifteen-hundred-dollar fee for a first-class plane ticket to visit my brother's film shoot to a fifteen-hundred-dollar fee for an all-day seminar with the marketer whom my brother was interviewing. When I thought of paying that much for a plane ticket, I was upset. When I thought of paying the same amount for the privilege of spending the day with a stellar marketer, I was enthused. The new thoughts were enough to transform my emotions.

Reassociations work most of the time, especially if you practice them. Sometimes, though, the mental act of reassociating isn't enough. In those cases, you need to do something physical to help shift your old negative emotion so that a new emotion takes its place. I call this principle *emotion for emotion*.

Here's a very simple example of emotion for emotion: You come home from work and find a huge credit card bill, far larger than you expected. You immediately begin worrying about how you're going to pay it. You sit down and make a budget, proving to yourself that you have a plan for taking care of this problem, but you still find yourself plagued with a feeling of unease.

"Why am I so bad with money?" you think. "What if I overspend again next month—how will I take care of it then? What if this plan doesn't work and I can't pay the bill off so quickly? What if other expenses come up and I run short of money in a more serious way? What if . . . what if . . . what if . . .?" Before you know it, you've pictured yourself homeless and penniless, reduced to poverty, and even though you *know* this is an irrational fear, you can't seem to shake the anxiety.

You try to create a reassociation. Instead of associating an unpaid bill with the prospect of financial doom, why not associate it with something positive, you think, with confidence in your financial future ("I can't pay the bill now, but I will be able to pay it later") or pleasure in the things you bought with the money? Nothing works. In fact, trying to reassociate only makes you feel more anxious. Besides feeling fear, you feel guilt, shame, and self-hatred.

At this point, you should probably start trying to trade emotion for emotion. Instead of thinking your way out of the problem, simply substitute a different emotion for the feeling of fear. To create the new emotion, engage in a new activity. Here are some suggestions:

- Take a brisk walk, go for a run, or do a vigorous workout.
- Go for a stroll somewhere beautiful, soothing, exciting, or interesting.
- Meditate for five to ten minutes, with the intention of quieting your mind.

- Take a warm, soothing bath or a brisk shower.
- Call a friend and force yourself to talk about a completely different subject, one that absorbs your interest.
- Play with an animal or a child.
- Tend to your plants. Ideally, you would do more than water them; remove dead leaves, prune or fertilize them, or even get out the mister and make sure they have all the moisture they need.
- Do the dishes, run the vacuum cleaner, or get involved in some other household chore.

You get the idea. Find something absorbing to do, and your emotions will shift as your attention does. Doing these physical activities takes you out of the fear of "what if" and allows you to feel a positive emotion. You are not feeling more internal and are in a better place to make a good decision of what your next steps will be. Most of the things we worry about never come to pass anyway. Trading the emotion of anxiety, fear, and scarcity for more positive emotions of peace, exuberance, and enthusiasm by doing something physical will give you the mental strength to address your situation with another perspective. Have you ever done a jigsaw puzzle and just got stuck? You *could* find the right piece. You took a break and did something else for a moment and then when you came back to the puzzle you seemed to find the piece you were looking for. Trading emotion for emotion does just that. It allows you to step away from the external world offending your emotional fingerprint and allows you to internally realign yourself to take on any task, challenge, or situation. For additional ideas on activities you can do to trade emotion for emotion based on each aspect of your emotional fingerprint, refer to the last section of chapter 6, "Creating Internal Validations."

When Your Path Is Clear

The wonderful thing about clearing your path is that you don't know where that open road will take you. Maybe you'll fulfill your dream and maximize a previously ignored aspect of your emotional fingerprint. Perhaps you'll give up your current dream and find a new one, or maybe you'll wander around, apparently to no purpose, and then discover that all this time you've been heading toward a success that you recognize only when you get there.

To inspire you, I leave you with this quote from educator, philosopher, and civil rights leader Howard Thurman, the spiritual adviser to Dr. Martin Luther King Jr.: "Don't ask yourself what the world needs; ask yourself what makes you come alive. And then go and do that. Because what the world needs is people who have come alive."

What makes you come alive, of course, is what makes you feel important. When you are maximizing your emotional fingerprint, you feel fully alive and engaged in your life. Clearing your path of fear can help you to reach that joyous state. So can clarifying your standards, which is the topic of the next chapter.

8

Clarify Your Standards

I've learned that people will forget what you said,
people will forget what you did, but people will
never forget how you made them feel.

—Maya Angelou

When my wife and I got married, I had a mental list of what I thought a wife should be. I loved her, and I knew that she loved me, but that didn't really affect my expectations. I wanted her to be more free-spirited, more spontaneous, less worried about money, and less concerned with planning every little thing. Looking back on it now, I think I probably wanted her to be more like me!

My wife had her own expectations for me. She wanted me to be more careful, to call if I was going to be late, to be more thrifty, and to be a better planner. She probably wished I was more like her!

Because we had such strong expectations for each other and the relationship, we often found ourselves clashing. "Why didn't you pick up your towel off the floor?" "Why can't we ever just go out on the spur of the moment?" "Why didn't you bring me dinner in bed? You know I'm sick!" "How come you woke me up this morning? You know I like to stay up late and sleep in!" We never stopped loving each other, but we sure were having a lot of disagreements.

Then one day, about five years ago, a miracle happened—the one that I had been waiting for throughout our entire marriage. Finally, my wife became perfect!

How did this happen? It wasn't because she had suddenly changed; it was because I had finally stopped wanting her to meet my expectations.

Expectations versus Standards

Many of my clients get hung up on the crucial question of expectations versus standards. They are excited to learn about the emotional fingerprints, and they feel empowered when they learn to internalize and validate them and take control of their lives.

When things don't go the way they expected, however, they feel frustrated. "If I'm truly in control of my life, then my life should go the way I want it to," my client Mara told me. "Isn't that the point?"

Actually, that isn't the point, any more than my wife living up to my expectations was the point of our marriage. We can work hard at making our personal lives, our relationships, and our work lives the way we want them to be, and sometimes we'll succeed. My wife can sometimes get me to pick up the towels. I can sometimes get her to drop the detailed schedule she's planned for herself and go on a spontaneous excursion with me. Mara, who was working hard to start her own business as a public relations consultant, was sometimes able to make the deals she wanted with the clients she wanted, and she was sometimes able to hire the copywriters and the designers she wanted at the prices she wanted.

Then one day, there I am, dropping the towels on the floor again, and there's my wife, sticking stubbornly to her own schedule. There's Mara's client, switching the deadline on her at the last minute; her favorite copywriter just called in sick with the flu, and her favorite designer has decided to move to Buenos Aires. At that moment, life has not given any of us what we wanted, and there's just not that much that we can do about it.

Does that mean we've failed? If we're looking at expectations, yes. If we're looking at standards, not at all.

Expectations Are External, Standards Are Internal

Expectations are, by definition, external. They concern an external reality that we simply can't control and that will by necessity disappoint us, at least some of the time. If we try to maximize our emotional fingerprints by making our expectations come true, we are dooming ourselves to failure.

If Mara expects a client to follow a schedule, for example, she has given control of her happiness over to that client. She'll be happy when he meets her expectations and unhappy when he doesn't.

Likewise, if my wife expects me to pick up the towels, she'll be happy when I do so and unhappy when I don't. Her expectations of me have put her in my power. I can make her happy when I meet them and unhappy when I don't. Similarly, if I expect her to behave spontaneously with me, she has the power to make me happy by meeting my expectations and the power to make me unhappy by failing to meet them.

Standards, in contrast, are internal. They are what we ask of ourselves, not what we expect of anyone else. If Mara defines her business success by the behavior of her clients and her employees, she'll often be disappointed—and there will be very little she can do to prevent that. If she instead defines her success by her *own* behavior—that is, if she lives up to her own standards for being fair, punctual, dedicated, and 100 percent committed to her clients' projects—then it is *always* within her power to be successful. She may not always be able to make her clients happy, and her clients may not always make her happy, but Mara can always make *herself* happy, if she is basing her life on standards rather than expectations.

I can choose to let my wife make me happy by behaving spontaneously and make me unhappy by insisting on sticking to her schedule. If that's how I'm judging our marriage, then our relationship is a success when my wife is meeting my expectations and a failure when she chooses not to. If instead I choose to define my marriage by my own standards, then our relationship is a success when I decide that my wife is someone I want to remain married to and when I treat her in a loving, generous, and respectful way.

It is always in my power to decide whether our marriage is up to my standards. It is always in my power to treat my wife according to my standards. That's why our relationship improved so much when I let go of my expectations. If I am focusing on expectations, I need my wife to behave in a certain way, and I'm always trying to "fix" her when she's not behaving that way. If I'm focusing on standards, I look at my *own* behavior whenever anything goes wrong. I decide whether I'm living up to my own standards, and if I'm not, I put my efforts into my own behavior without trying to alter my wife's.

I do ask myself whether my marriage is up to my standards—whether I am in a good, loving relationship rather than a neglectful or an abusive one—but this is a very different question from whether my wife is meeting my expectations (especially since, in fifteen years of marriage, I don't think she has ever met one!).

This is a crucial point for maximizing your emotional fingerprint. If you try to do it by meeting your expectations or getting others to meet them, you will often find yourself failing. If you try to maximize your emotional fingerprint by developing your own standards and then trying to meet them, you will always have it in your power to succeed. Even if your relationship fails, you can always meet your own standards by choosing to leave it. When you focus on meeting your own standards, your are much more likely to succeed in your relationships, your business, and your personal life.

Examples of Expectations
Personal Life

1. I expect to live in a nice house.
2. I expect to get along well with my family.
3. I expect to have lots of close friends whom I see often.

Relationships

1. I expect to be married to a person who makes me happy.
2. I expect to have a healthy intimate life with my partner.
3. I expect to have my partner's love and support.

Work Life

1. I expect to make a lot of money.
2. I expect to have a job in which I delegate the worst tasks to someone else.
3. I expect my boss and my coworkers to treat me with respect.

Examples of Standards

Personal Life

1. I will create a warm, pleasant, and welcoming environment wherever I live.
2. I will keep my heart open to my family members and be available for whatever level of warm and close relationships they will go along with.
3. I will be a loving, loyal, and generous friend.

Relationships

1. Whether I am married, dating, or "just looking," I will extend myself to find ways to make my love interest happy, and I welcome the possibility of deepening our commitment.
2. I will be a generous and an attentive lover.
3. I will fully and freely offer my love and support.

Work Life

1. I will work hard and faithfully at whatever job I take on.
2. I will identify what I love to do most, commit to doing it well, and seek opportunities to do as much of it as possible and as often as possible.
3. I will offer respect to everyone I work with.

Notice how the expectations are entirely outside your control. You could do some things to try to get those expectations met, and some of the time you might succeed, but they are never 100 percent within your control.

The standards, in contrast, are entirely within your control. You might not always live up to your standards—I've never met a human being who didn't slip at least some of the time—but doing so is always within your control. Having expectations can be an exercise in frustration as you ride the emotional roller coaster of having them met at times and not met at other times. Having standards is an exercise in growth as you work toward becoming your best self.

Focusing on standards rather than on expectations is therefore the key to maximizing your emotional fingerprint in your personal life, your relationships, and your work life.

EXERCISE

Turning Expectations into Standards

1. Identify some of your expectations by completing the following chart.

   In my personal life, I expect

   _____

   _____

   In my relationships, I expect

   _____

   _____

   In my work life, I expect

   _____

   _____

2. Now experiment with turning those expectations into standards. How could you reframe your external expectations so as to create internal standards that are within your control to attain?

In my personal life, I will

_____

_____

In my relationships, I will

_____

_____

In my work life, I will

_____

_____

Expectations without Implementation = Frustration

My sons, Hunter and Pierce, whom I introduced in an earlier chapter, are both good kids. Most of the time they try to do the right thing, and I couldn't be prouder of them.

Sometimes, though, they drive me up a wall. They won't pick up after themselves until my wife and I remind them. They aren't always ready to leave for school when I am ready to take them. They won't keep their Legos off the floor and out of my way. In short, they won't stop acting like kids.

When I find myself getting frustrated with them, I have to stop and ask myself: Is this a question of standards or expectations?

Standards are clearly set out ahead of time, they are agreed on by both parties, and the associated rewards and punishments are also known and agreed on. When you get a driver's license, for example, you agree to follow the driving laws of whatever part of the country you're in. The speed limit is clearly posted. The reward of following the speed limit is that you are allowed to keep driving. The penalty of breaking the speed limit is paying a fine, and if you break the limit often enough, you might lose your license or even go to jail.

These are not expectations; they are standards. You know what you have to do, and you know what will happen if you don't. You agreed to those conditions when you signed up for a driver's license, and you're unlikely to be surprised if a police officer or a judge demands that you meet them.

Imagine if there were no posted speed limits for a given stretch of road. You see some other signs: Children Playing, Slippery When Wet, Bridge May Be Icy in Cold Weather. Other than that, there is no indication of how fast you are allowed to drive, so you assume that it's okay to do whatever seems right to you.

Suddenly you hear a siren behind you, and a police officer pulls you over. She explains that she's giving you a speeding ticket and names a fine.

"Wait a minute," you say. "First, my friend Dave got a ticket last week, and he had to pay only half that much. Second, I don't see why I'm paying a ticket at all. No speed limit was posted, so I just followed my own judgment."

"Yes, but you obviously have terrible judgment!" the officer replies. "I expect you to understand that when you see the Children Playing sign, you slow down to twenty miles per hour, and when you see that the bridge may be icy, you slow down to ten miles per hour."

"How can I understand that?" you ask reasonably. "I had no way of knowing that *that's* what that sign meant. I did slow down—but to twenty-five miles per hour, not twenty, and I honked my horn loudly to let the kids know to get out of the way. In my opinion, I behaved perfectly, and you shouldn't give me any penalty."

"What kind of person would think that?" says the officer. "No reasonable driver would interpret the sign that way. It isn't logical. However, tomorrow, I might change my mind about what Children Playing happens to mean. The next police officer you encounter may have a different interpretation of the rules. And we might change the penalty for breaking the rules without ever telling you about it. Here's your ticket! Have a nice day!"

Without a posted, clearly marked speed limit, standards disappear. No longer are drivers operating according to clear, measurable principles on which everyone has agreed. Instead, each driver is expected to somehow meet each police officer's expectations. As a result, you're often not sure what the expectations are, who has them, and whether they are subject to change.

Moreover, the officer is looking to punish you because you didn't implement her expectations. Expectations require implementation. Expectations without implementation equals frustration. Because the officer has expectations rather than standards, she is going to impose them on you and punish you for not meeting them.

How often does this happen to you, and how often do you do it to others in your personal life, your relationships, and your work life? Take a look at the following list of expectation statements and ask yourself how often you've said them and how you feel when you hear them.

Expectation Statements

"If you loved me, you'd know . . . "

"Any reasonable person would do it that way."

"I didn't think I *had* to explain."

"Who *does* that? No one!"

"You're old enough to understand that . . ."

"This is not the kind of work our department expects."

"You of all people should know that . . ."

"How could you possibly think that?"

When I start feeling frustrated with my sons, it's almost always because they are not implementing my expectations of them. I expect them to pick up after themselves. I expect them to be ready to leave on time for school. I expect them to be polite and considerate. It doesn't really matter whether these expectations are good or bad, realistic or unrealistic, healthy or unhealthy. Having them is a recipe for frustration, because every time one of my kids doesn't implement them, for whatever reason, I'm going to be angry or disappointed. That's the nature of expectations.

Standards, in contrast, don't have that built-in component of frustration, because they, along with the rewards and punishments, have been agreed on by all parties. Standards are your way of setting boundaries, negotiating, and coming to an agreement. Giving up expectations doesn't mean that the other person gets to do whatever he or she wants with no consequences. It just means that everyone has agreed on some common standards, and the relationship proceeds on that basis.

If you'd like to contrast how frustrating expectations can be with how satisfying standards often are, see the following table.

Frustrating Expectations versus Satisfying Standards

Frustrating Expectations	Satisfying Standards
You should drop everything if your parents or siblings need your help.	I look at my family's needs and requests, and I make my own decisions about what is reasonable, what I'm willing to do, and what fits my own standards for a loving member of my family.
You should attend all family dinners and celebrations.	I ask questions to find out how important a particular celebration is to other family members, then I make my own decisions about balancing family obligations with other things I care about.
You should be available to talk when I really need you.	We agree, as friends, that we'll each be clear about how urgent our needs are. We agree to respect each other's limits and understand that we can't always do everything we might like.
You should care about being on time as much as I do.	I understand that being on time is very important to you. Even though it's not such a big deal to me, I'll accommodate you by being on time for our meetings.
If you loved me, you'd know how to make me happy.	I will tell you what's important to me so that you know how to make me happy. I will try hard to make you happy, based on what's important to you.
If you loved me, you'd want to have sex as often as I do, in the way that I do.	We agree to take each other's sexual needs and preferences into account.

Frustrating Expectations	Satisfying Standards
You should work evenings and weekends whenever necessary, without complaining.	We agree ahead of time on what the company policy is for overtime and extra work. I will take the job or not take the job based on whether I want to comply with that policy.
I should be earning a certain amount of money by now.	I will make a realistic plan to get the income I want, and I'll take actions to fulfill it.
I should be at a certain level of promotion (partner, senior management) by now.	I will make a realistic plan to get the level of career success I want, and I'll take actions to fulfill it.

As you can see from the chart, sometimes standards are for *yourself*—what you'll do to meet your own goals or to give another person pleasure—and sometimes standards are for *a relationship:* what you want to be able to count on with a friend, a family member, or a romantic partner or in a work situation. If a friendship, a marriage, or a job is not up to your standards—if you consider it abusive, one-sided, or simply unfulfilling—you may take steps to change it or decide to leave. In all cases, your focus is on yourself, what you are and are not willing to do, not on how you want another person to change.

In our house, things went a lot smoother when we all agreed that if the boys were ready by 7:55 a.m., I would give them a ride to school. If they weren't ready, they would walk. I wasn't trying to impose my expectations on them; instead, we all agreed on a common standard. Some days my sons are ready on time; some days they aren't. Either way, I don't have to get frustrated, because the standard is recognized.

Likewise, with speed limits, we've all agreed that if I keep breaking the speed limit, a series of known punishments will occur. First I'll get a ticket or two, then I'll get a larger fine, and then I'll lose my license. I know where I stand, and so does everyone involved in enforcing the law. No frustration is necessary.

Having standards rather than expectations is the key to maximizing your emotional fingerprint. If you have expectations, you're like the greyhound who chases the mechanical rabbit: you'll never really be able to catch your prey, because the possibility always exists for other people and even life itself to slip out of your control. Your expectations will often not be met, and you'll never really be in charge of when they *are* met.

If you have standards, in contrast, you're like the greyhound who stops running and makes a 180-degree turn. Suddenly you have something concrete to work toward: meeting your own standards and coming to an agreement with others on commonly held standards. It's as though the mechanical rabbit stopped running away from you and is now running toward you. Maximizing your emotional fingerprint is no longer an impossible goal but something that is always within your power.

EXERCISE

Implementation and Frustration

Think of a recent incident that frustrated you.

_____

_____

What expectations did you have in that situation?

_____

_____

How were your expectations not met?

_____

_____

Can you imagine a way to turn your past expectations into standards?

_____

_____

Desired Outcomes versus Positive Outcomes

Mara was still not completely on board with my distinction between expectations and standards. She kept telling me about all of the things she was doing in her new business to ensure that her expectations were met. She seemed to think that if she visualized exactly what she wanted and was willing to work hard, she could guarantee the outcomes she wanted. She didn't understand that maximizing her emotional fingerprint is always an *internal* exercise.

You can't control anything but yourself. Maximizing your emotional fingerprint is not about getting other people to do things your way or making them conform to your expectations. It's about having your own standards and living up to them.

I tried to help Mara see this by introducing a related concept: desired outcomes versus positive outcomes. Like the greyhound with the mechanical rabbit, you can chase desired outcomes all you like, but you can never guarantee them. Sooner or later, some aspect of your results will fail to live up to your hopes and expectations, and you'll have to accept that an important component of your life is out of your control. A loved one may break up with you or even die. A business may fail. A hobby may simply stop being interesting to you, or you may become physically unable to pursue it, leaving a void that has not yet been filled. These are not the outcomes you desire.

If you have internalized your emotional fingerprint, however, you can make any outcome into a positive outcome. You can even take a tragedy, learn from it, and create something positive by the way you respond.

Stephani Victor was an aspiring actress and filmmaker when she was struck down in a horrific automobile accident. To save her life, the doctors amputated both of her legs, which would seem to have put an end to Stephani's hopes and dreams. In no way did this accident have any place on the list of Stephani's desired outcomes.

Nevertheless, Stephani found several extraordinary ways to create positive outcomes from this potentially tragic situation. She made a documentary about her experience, which offered her a route back to filmmaking and on-camera work. She found other ways to make films and to appear on screen. She even decided to become a skier in the Paralympics, an international athletic competition for the disabled. Today she has numerous trophies, gold medals, and World Cups from the Paralympics, demonstrating how much she has forged a positive outcome out of an undesired one.

Stephani is an example of how you can work through any tragedy when you are in touch with what truly makes you feel important—when you understand your emotional fingerprint. Having identified what made her feel important, Stephani developed enormous emotional reserves by internalizing her emotional fingerprint rather than pursuing it externally. Then she cleared her path of obstacles and clarified her standards. She maximized her emotional fingerprint because she let go of her expectations—to become an actress and a filmmaker in a whole and healthy body—and focused instead on her standards: to be a woman of courage who defined her goals and would not be stopped in her pursuit of them.

EXERCISE

Exploring Outcomes

1. Identify three situations in which you did *not* get the outcome that you wanted. Choose one situation from your personal life, one from your relationships, and one from your work life.

   Undesired outcome in personal life:

   _____

   _____

   Undesired outcome in relationships:

   _____

   _____

   Undesired outcome in work life:

   _____

   _____

2. Identify at least one way to turn that undesired outcome into a positive outcome through the way you internalize and then maximize your emotional fingerprint.

Personal life:

_____

_____

Relationships:

_____

_____

Work life:

_____

_____

Excitement versus Enthusiasm

Every great and commanding moment in the annals of the world is
the triumph of some enthusiasm.

—Ralph Waldo Emerson

The crowded hallway emptied as a young man walked along in
isolated frustration. Another semester had passed, and he was no
closer to his goals. He had applied many times to be accepted into
the elite program that offered a degree in animation, but to no avail.
He had been rejected again.

Doug's lifelong passion was to be an animator for Hollywood
films. To that end, his university schedule was filled with courses in
art, computer rendering, and live animations, and he was doing well
in all of his classes. Yet he had never been officially admitted to the
program that would allow him to graduate as an accredited animator.

Only twenty people a year were allowed into that program,
and Doug was never one of them. Finally, he made a decision: he
would take all of the courses in the program even though he hadn't
formally been admitted to it. He could do the actual coursework,
but it would be credited only as general education and would not
count toward his desired major. He would have the knowledge but
not the recognition.

Doug threw himself into every course, working nights and weekends and even over the summer. Many of the classes were set up for students to work in teams, completing projects that could not be done alone. Doug's classmates—who *had* been accepted into the program—were struck by his enthusiasm, which soon made Doug a very popular team member. No one realized that Doug wasn't an actual member of the program. They only saw his passion for the work.

Eventually, though, Doug's classmates found out his secret. Then a remarkable thing happened. Although you might think that students in a highly selective program would be happy to keep their competition out, Doug's classmates actually petitioned for his admittance into the program.

Initially, Doug was rejected again, even though by this point he had been attending class for three years. Finally, after working on multiple senior projects, Doug was accepted into the animation program during his last year of school, winning him the chance to present his work to some of the top studios in the world.

Doug's first internship was at EA Sports, a video game manufacturer. His world changed when he got a call from Pixar Studios. A lifetime of enthusiasm for his work had brought him to this moment. If you ever watch Disney/Pixar's extremely popular movie *Up*, you will see his name, Doug Rigby, in the credits.

Doug's story is a testament to the power of enthusiasm, which I see as the feeling you get when you are passionately validating your emotional fingerprint internally. Enthusiasm is a self-generating kind of pleasure that springs from a very deep place—the same place that produces your sense of importance. If you look at your emotional fingerprint, you will see that a natural enthusiasm wells up every time you find a way to internalize one of your seven aspects of importance. Every activity or relationship that helps you to feel important creates enthusiasm.

Enthusiasm, in turn, is the fuel that energizes you, enabling you to maximize your emotional fingerprint. If, like Doug, you are enthusiastic about an activity, a topic, or a person, your natural passion will communicate itself to others, opening doors and creating opportunities. More important, you will find within your-self a constant, self-replenishing source of joy.

Another way to describe enthusiasm is to say that it is the result of honoring your standards. When you are in a personal situation, a relationship, or a work situation that meets your standards, you have reason to be enthusiastic. When you are engaged in an activity that honors your standards—with friends, family, your partner, or at work—you have even more reason to be enthusiastic.

In contrast, excitement is an external source of pleasure and therefore unreliable by nature. It's like a caffeinated energy drink: while the effects last, you feel jazzed, hyped, and ready for any-thing, but after a few hours, your energy high is followed by an energy crash and you're left needing another fix. Like the grey-hound chasing the mechanical rabbit on the track, you can never really stop running.

Think of the first new car you bought. It had that new-car smell, you were proud of it and showed it to all of your friends, and just driving it was really exciting. Then the first time you went through the drive-through window of your favorite burger joint, the new-car smell was gone. Within a couple of months, you were frus-trated by the monthly payment and the maintenance fees. Finally, you weren't excited about the car any longer. You either had to have a new possession or start looking forward to the next new car. You weren't asking whether your car continued to meet your stan-dards for what you want in a car and whether you had reason to be grateful and enthusiastic for owning such a useful item. Instead, you were frustrated that your car didn't meet your expectations for ongoing excitement.

The same can be true in your relationships. When you first meet someone special, you feel a rush of excitement, leading to such emotional highs as your first kiss and your first "I love you." The excitement is really going now, and you stay up all night talking. You are convinced you would do anything for this person. He or she is present in all of your thoughts. At that moment, you feel that the other person is meeting all of your expectations, or at least most of them.

Over time, however, the thrill wears off, and most of the excitement fades. You begin to see how the other person is failing to meet first one expectation, then another. The whole relationship is probably failing to meet your expectation of generating constant excitement. So if your main interest *was* excitement, the relationship is over for you. You feel a need to move on to the next relationship in order to maintain excitement, just as you need to reach for the next energy drink in order to maintain a buzz.

The pattern is the same in a career. At first a new job brings new pay, new projects, and great opportunities. The job is either meeting most of your expectations or seems as though it soon will. Then you become accustomed to the new reality and realize that it is all just more work. You aren't asking yourself whether the job meets your standards for what you need from it or whether you are honoring your standards and taking pleasure in the kind of worker you are. Instead, you're looking for something to fulfill your expectations—and you are, inevitably, disappointed.

Unless you have internal reasons to be enthusiastic about a possession, a daily activity, a relationship, or a type of work, you will find yourself frustrated when the excitement wears off—and believe me, it *always* wears off. Because excitement is external, it always has a natural limit.

In contrast, enthusiasm is internal, and it is closely related to standards. When you are clear about what you value and what you desire, you pursue the activities and relationships that make you feel important, and you experience an ongoing sense of joy as a result. The pleasure comes from internalizing your emotional fingerprint—from finding your own internal reasons to be happy and proud, regardless of external outcomes and results.

When you fail to clarify your standards, you fall prey to expectations: the outcomes that you would *like* to see but that are never fully in your control. Excitement and fear are siblings: you feel excited when you sense a potential gain; you feel fear when you sense a potential loss. Both feelings put you at the mercy of external events and results that are by definition outside your control.

When Stephani won her first gold medal in the Paralympics, she was overcome with excitement. When I interviewed her about the experience several years later, she told me that she had not been at all prepared for the emotional letdown afterward. The excitement was over. The chase of a seven-year saga had come to an end. She was so upset by how low she felt that she even called the president of the Paralympics to say that the organization should provide counseling for its athletes, because having proved she was the best in the world, she now had no idea what to do next.

I had a similar experience early in my career. I had just spoken to a crowd in a sold-out venue, and I was on top of the world. The event was picture-perfect: I got a standing ovation, people formed a long line to sign up for my coaching programs, and the event promoter was thrilled with the results. The next morning, however, I woke up feeling miserable. My wife and I talked it over. I was so frustrated. Here it was, Saturday morning, and I was about to mow the lawn, whereas just twelve hours earlier I had been the toast of the town.

My wife pointed out to me that I had been excited about the event but not enthused. My focus had been entirely on the results I got and the responses of others, so when those results wore off and the responses faded away, I was left wanting more. From that point on I decided to be enthused instead of excited about what I do. I would focus not on the results I achieved but on the standards I set for myself and my work.

If I met my own standards, I would be happy. If I didn't, I would work harder to meet them the next time. If I found I was never meeting my standards, I would either revise my standards or change my approach to my work. In all of these cases, my focus would be on the love and passion I feel for the work itself—an endlessly renewable source of enthusiasm. Since there are always opportunities to do my work, I never need to feel let down. The joy of doing what makes me feel important is always available to me. It was now always within my power to maximize my emotional fingerprint.

As you can see, maximizing your emotional fingerprint means letting go of fear, expectations, and excitement and focusing on intentions, standards, and enthusiasm. One dictionary definition of *enthusiasm* is "the action of being inspired by God from within, absorbing or controlling possession of the mind by any interest or pursuit." In contrast, *excitement* is "to rouse to an emotional response, to stir to action, to provoke, to stir up, to stimulate." Which would you rather have as a constant companion in your life?

Think about what your week is like when you are chasing excitement. On Monday you may be excited to watch your favorite reality show, but when your favorite contestant gets kicked off, you feel disappointed. On Tuesday you may be afraid that your boss or your spouse won't acknowledge you for a job well done. If you get the response you expected, you are excited; if these important people in your life don't meet your expectations, you are frustrated or disappointed. On Wednesday, you might be excited to get ready for the weekend trip coming up, but you may also be fearful about whether the trip will go well. Either it won't meet your expectations and you'll be disappointed or the trip will meet your expectations perfectly and then hit you with a big emotional letdown when it is over. Day after day, month after month, you are always chasing the mechanical rabbit, never satisfied with where you already are.

Enthusiasm is different. It is the action of being inspired from within. On Monday you might feel enthusiastic for the day because your work presentation is complete, and regardless of the outcome, you know you did a great job. You are looking not at your expectations for how your boss might respond but at your standards for how you behaved and what you achieved. On Tuesday you could be grateful and enthusiastic for where you are in your life, because you see that your romantic relationship fits your standards and you are happy with your own decisions. On Wednesday, because you are focused on your standards, you live in the moment and are not worried about the outcome. No one is required to meet your expectations, so no one can let you down. You are focused on your standards, and you are free to feel enthusiastic about honoring them. That's the way to maximize your emotional fingerprint.

Learning to Distinguish between Excitement and Enthusiasm

Use my example as a guide to filling in the questions that follow:

1. Identify a situation in your life in which you felt excited and then let down.

   I spent a ridiculous amount of money on a film project about the emotional fingerprint, thinking it would be an overnight success.

2. Identify the expectations you held in that situation.
   - I thought my film would have a similar success as the film *The Secret*, which was about the law of attraction.
   - I expected it to launch my career to another level.
   - I expected to make my money back in the first year after the film was completed.

3. Internalize your emotional fingerprint by identifying how you might convert each of those expectations to a standard and then honor that standard.
   - The standard would be to make a movie that honors the integrity of my message. I did honor that standard, but I expected a different outcome. If I would use my standard as my measuring stick, then I would say the movie was a complete success.
   - The standard would be to call thirty retail outlets in ninety days to get them to carry the DVD. That would have been in my control.
   - The standard would be to accept that I had invested the money for long-term success and not look for an immediate return on my investment.

4. Identify a situation in your life in which you feel or might feel enthusiastic.

   I feel enthusiastic about sharing with the world the message of how to internalize the emotional fingerprint.

5. Explain how you will keep the enthusiasm going by internalizing your emotional fingerprint and honoring your standards.

No longer do I measure my success by external results. I know when the work I have shared has affected someone's life. I will set a standard that once a week I will coach someone in need for free. When my children get older, if they want to be part of the business, I will show them how I do what I do. This is my life's work. I have no desire to retire. I will always pursue this passion with a full purpose of heart.

Now it's your turn.

1. Identify a situation in your life in which you felt excited and then let down.

    _____

    _____

2. Identify the expectations you held in that situation.

    _____

    _____

3. Internalize your emotional fingerprint by identifying how you might convert each of those expectations to a standard and then honor that standard.

    _____

    _____

4. Identify a situation in your life in which you feel or might feel enthusiastic.

    _____

    _____

5. Explain how you will keep the enthusiasm going by internalizing your emotional fingerprint and honoring your standards.

    _____

    _____

Changing Your Dreams

When Conrad was growing up, he wanted to be like his dad. His father was a successful entrepreneur who owned many businesses in their small town, and everyone could see that he was an important man.

It wasn't easy for young Conrad, though. His father rarely supported him and often told him what an unsatisfactory son he was. One morning, when Conrad's father found his son sleeping past seven o'clock, he called him a "lazy oaf who would never amount to anything."

Conrad began a long search for the success that would prove his father wrong. He entered politics and won a seat in New Mexico's state legislature. After serving two years, he persuaded his father to open a bank with him. He started as a teller, and within a couple of years he had worked his way up to being president. Wanting to break out on his own, he looked for a bank to buy. At last, he believed, his dreams of independence and success were about to come true.

Conrad had enough connections in the banking industry to borrow the money, and he had also saved some of his own. After just missing two opportunities to buy small banks, he went to Cisco, Texas, where another bank was for sale. This time, because he had been outbid in the other two sales, Conrad chose not to negotiate but simply paid the first price he was given. However, the seller took that speedy acceptance as an indication that he had set the price too low, so he raised the price.

Frustrated, Conrad realized that he would have to stay longer to continue the negotiations. He went to the local hotel to find a room. Observing the bustling lobby, he asked the owner how business was. The owner told him that the hotel was indeed doing well, but he was tired of the hospitality trade and wanted to get into oil, which in that part of Texas was clearly a profitable enterprise.

By the end of that day, Conrad Hilton was the proud owner of his first hotel—and on his way to building the giant corporation that would make him a household name. He never did realize his dream of owning a bank. Life offered him the chance to change his dream, and he took it.

Sometimes you can't get the dream you *think* you want, but a new opportunity offers you the chance for an even more satisfying dream. You might miss the opportunity, though, if you're focused on expectations, desired outcomes, and excitement. In order to take advantage of all of the wonderful possibilities that life makes available, you need to internalize your emotional fingerprint, stay in touch with your standards, and be open to any chance for enthusiasm. If you're focused on your expectations, you'll see only what you're looking for. If you're grounded in your standards, you'll tap into your natural passion and enthusiasm for any opportunity that might make you feel important.

Standards and the Emotional Fingerprint

Here's the funny thing about expectations: they are often nothing more than standards turned inside out. We often begin with our standards for ourselves and then expect other people to hold them as dearly as we do.

This is related to the way that we often attribute our own aspects of importance to other people. I feel important when I am free and independent, so I assume that everyone else does, too. That's why it's so frustrating when my wife wants to plan or schedule activities. I simply can't understand why she doesn't have the same emotional fingerprint that I do—or why she doesn't hold the same standards. I judge almost every relationship and situation based on whether it allows me the freedom and independence that I need. That is my standard. My wife has quite different standards. When I expect her to meet my standards—especially if I expect her to *share* my standards—that's a recipe for frustration.

Of course, my wife and I do share *some* standards, particularly for our relationship. It's important to both of us that we love and respect each other, that we maintain fidelity, that we put parenting ahead of all other responsibilities, and that we support each other on our separate paths as well as in our relationship. Those principles are like the agreed-on "speed limit" in our relationship. It's understood that these are the standards for our relationship.

If either of us were to violate these standards, the consequences would be terrible. When both of us honor these standards, our relationship is great—especially since we are now no longer trying to "fix" each other or get one to meet the other's expectations. Now when there's a relationship problem, I turn to my emotional fingerprint and my personal standards. What can *I* do to validate my emotional fingerprint? How do I meet my *own* standards? Focusing on these issues makes me a far better husband and father, and I end up feeling far happier with my wife.

In order to meet your own standards, you have to know what they are. Once again, it all comes back to your emotional fingerprint. Ultimately, your standards are the principles that help you to validate all of your aspects of importance. Let me take you through it step-by-step.

1. Identify your emotional fingerprint.

   Here's my list:

   1. Being connected to God, spirit, or the universe
   2. Providing
   3. Being free and independent
   4. Being creative
   5. Achieving my life's purpose
   6. Being a good parent
   7. Experiencing life

   Write your list:

   1. _____
   2. _____
   3. _____
   4. _____
   5. _____
   6. _____
   7. _____

2. For each aspect of your emotional fingerprint, identify a standard that will help you to validate that aspect.

   Here's my list:

   1. Strive every day to read the scriptures and have meaningful prayers.

2. Strive to provide emotional, physical, mental, spiritual, and financial stability to my family and friends.
3. Designate at least fifteen minutes a day to doing something that makes me feel free and independent.
4. Find art and sculpture that inspires me.
5. Live with integrity as I pursue my life's purpose.
6. Let my kids know that I love them no matter what they do.
7. Treat my mind and my body with respect so that I can fully experience life.

Write your list:

1. _____
2. _____
3. _____
4. _____
5. _____
6. _____
7. _____

If you want a relationship of any kind to really take off, do this exercise with that person and identify each other's standards. Then have a good talk about the standards that you have in common. Identify the punishments if you don't meet those standards as well as the rewards you can expect if you do. Maybe, like my wife and I, you'll suddenly discover that the other person in the relationship has been pretty close to perfect all along.

9

Sharpen Your Resolve

Man's mind, once stretched by a new idea, never
regains its original dimensions.
—Oliver Wendell Holmes

Recently, my wife wanted to have a garage sale. This kind
of activity is something she loves, but I can't understand
why it means so much to her. It must appeal to her
aspects of importance of feeling free and independent and experiencing life, whereas for me, everything about holding a garage sale
seems to disrespect my aspects of feeling free and independent and
being creative. (This is especially interesting when you consider
that my wife and I both have the free and independent aspect
of importance, yet we interpret that aspect in opposite ways.)
Although she's very good at garage sales and easily makes several
hundred dollars every time she has one, I would rather see her
spend twice what she saves just to avoid having to spend *my*
Saturday on such a restrictive and uncreative activity.

As you can imagine, we've had a fight about this dozens of times
in our fifteen-year marriage. I've never won, but I have created some
unpleasant scenes and ruined some potentially enjoyable Saturday
nights. So this time I decided to do things a little differently.

First, I fully accepted how much I hated the idea of spending my Saturday afternoon involved in a garage sale. I didn't try to talk myself out of my negative feelings or berate myself for being a bad husband. I simply accepted my emotions.

Then I identified which aspects of my emotional fingerprint felt disrespected by the activity: primarily, feeling free and independent and being creative, although perhaps providing was also involved. After all, I make a good living and provide my family with everything it needs.

I asked myself whether there was a way that I could validate those aspects of importance myself and end this problem. Could I create a reassociation for the garage sale, as I had learned to do with the airfare (see chapter 6)?

I did manage to reassociate the garage sale from "a boring activity that wastes my time" to "an opportunity to give a generous gift to my wife by supporting her in something that makes her happy." That helped somewhat but not enough.

What about trading emotion for emotion, as we learned to do in chapter 7? Reassociations are a mental activity. Most of the time they work very well, but sometimes you need to trade emotion for emotion by getting involved in some kind of physical activity that helps you to shift your mood. The boys had been involved in a big baking project the night before, and our kitchen was still a mess. I rounded up Hunter and Pierce and got them to bring the dirty dishes over to the sink, where I began running some water to wash them. The activity helped some, but I was still frustrated by the idea of losing so much of my day to a ridiculous garage sale.

Would it help to shift my focus from expectations to standards, as we learned to do in chapter 8? I reminded myself that it was counterproductive to expect my wife to see the folly of garage sales, because, as we've seen, expectations are almost always a shortcut to frustration. In this case, given how often my wife and I have fought about this issue, it was downright silly to expect her to suddenly see the light and give up something that she had enjoyed for fifteen years. My standards required me to be generous and tolerant of this quirk of my wife's. After all, hadn't she put up with at least as many quirks of mine?

Reassociations, trading emotion for emotion, and focusing on my standards definitely helped, but in this case they weren't quite enough. I found myself asking the two questions that are the focus of this chapter:

1. What experience do I want to have?
2. What actions do I take to create that experience?

Just asking those questions was enough to produce an immediate, clear, and passionate pair of answers:

1. I wanted a pleasant Saturday with my family.
2. To create that experience, why didn't I focus on hanging out with my two sons in the kitchen rather than getting bent out of shape about what my wife was doing? Why didn't I organize a special date for me and my wife for that night, when the sale would be over, so I *could* enjoy her company, without having to endure a garage sale to do it?

This is exactly what I did. I had some special time with my sons and some special time with my wife, all because I had been conscious of my emotional fingerprint, internalized it, and maximized it.

I could so easily have reacted impulsively to my wife's garage sale. I could so easily have fought her, withdrawn emotionally, or otherwise conveyed to her how stupid I thought garage sales were.

Instead, I looked at the big picture and took the long view. I realized that I could certainly complain about my wife's activity, but that one afternoon of complaining could easily ruin both the afternoon *and* the evening—and perhaps the whole next day, too. I didn't have to feel trapped by her decision; there was plenty of room for me to have a happy day without interfering with her plans. I didn't have to feel that my creativity had been blocked; I could do something creative with my sons or by myself while she was organizing and conducting the sale. I sharpened my resolve to have a great day, and as a result, what could have been a bitter marital squabble ended up as a pleasant occasion for all of us. I had done it by reminding myself of what mattered to me most.

Keeping Your Eye on What
Matters to You Most

After clearing your path of fear and clarifying your standards, the final way to maximize your emotional fingerprint is to sharpen your resolve by homing in on what matters to you most. If you're going to make effective decisions in your personal life, your relationships, and your work life, it's crucial for you to have a clear idea of what matters and what doesn't.

Businesses do this by making very clear mission statements. They can't do everything; they can focus on one or two things that are the reason they went into business in the first place. To effectively fulfill their mission, they have to know what it is—as clearly and specifically as possible.

In relationships, sharpening your resolve is about knowing what's most important to you, whether you're seeking a new relationship or trying to improve a current one. One relationship can't be everything to you, and the other person can't be perfect. What's most important to you? If you're in a romantic relationship, what's worth making an issue of and what is better left alone? If you're seeking a romantic relationship, what are the most important qualities you want in a partner?

In your personal life, sharpening your resolve is about becoming very clear about what you're missing and being committed to getting it. Don't just say, "I want to have more fun." Are you looking for downtime that makes no demands on you, physical challenges, mental challenges, the opportunity to visit new places? Any of these things could be fun, but if you don't sharpen your resolve, you might not achieve any of them.

As you know, understanding your emotional fingerprint is the first step in knowing what you want and what's going to make you feel important. Internalizing your emotional fingerprint will help you to pursue what you want in an effective way that is guaranteed to succeed, because you're defining success in terms of who you are and what you can control. Maximizing your emotional fingerprint then helps you to make the most of your material, emotional, and spiritual resources in pursuit of your dreams, your goals, and the people you love. We've already seen how to clear your path and clarify your standards. Let's take a closer look at how to sharpen your resolve.

EXERCISE

Maximizing Your Emotional Fingerprint

Identify the three most important goals you have for each area of your life. These are the goals you'll be pursuing by maximizing your emotional fingerprint.

Use the example of Vanessa Serra, age forty, a divorced producer working in children's television, as a guide:

Personal Life

1. I want to spend time with my sister, Annette, who's struggling with breast cancer.
2. I want to spend some time in nature—at least once a week.
3. I'd like to get back to cooking for myself more—both for health reasons and for pleasure. Maybe also start a garden.

Relationships

1. I'm looking for a guy who knows how to laugh at himself when things get tough.
2. I want someone who likes to have fun and is not depressed.
3. I want someone who will respect my work, even if he doesn't like television.

Work Life

1. I want to create a stronger team at work—we don't pull together, and I want us to.
2. I want to move into more serious programs that could really help children.
3. I want to learn Japanese so I can see more of what the Japanese programs are like.

Now it's your turn.

Personal Life

1. _____

2. _____

3. _____

Relationships

1. _____

2. _____

3. _____

Work Life

1. _____

2. _____

3. _____

What Kind of Experience Do You Want?

We all live our lives second by second, minute by minute, and hour by hour, but most of those seconds, minutes, and hours are forgotten as soon as they pass. What we remember is not the two minutes it took to make a cup of coffee or the five hours we spent napping on a cross-country flight. We remember the experiences we create: the trip to Disneyland with the kids, the awful fight we had with our first boyfriend or girlfriend, or laughing till we cried at our favorite movie. We humans are continually creating experiences—good and bad, important and trivial, unusual and ordinary—and when we look back on our lives, we don't remember the individual minutes and seconds, we remember the experiences.

As we've seen throughout this book, the good experiences tend to be the ones that make us feel important by validating two or more aspects of importance of our emotional fingerprints.

The bad experiences tend to be the ones that make us feel unimportant by disrespecting two or more aspects of our emotional fingerprint. The more aspects an experience validates or disrespects, or the more intensely an experience affects two or more aspects, the more likely we are to remember it.

One of the best ways to sharpen your resolve, therefore, is to think about what kinds of experiences you want and then figure out what to do to create them. If you can master the ability to approach life in this way, you will really be able to own your life.

Think for a moment about how rare that approach is. It's far more common to drift along, either passively accepting the events of your life or reacting unconsciously to try to change them.

Suppose a man is rushing through his morning as he prepares for work. He's already stressed out by thoughts of his demanding boss and his mounting pile of work, so when his five-year-old son spills the milk, he doesn't see the child who's doing the best he can, he sees only one more obstacle.

"Why can't you be more careful?" he snaps, and the child withdraws, cries, or answers back, none of which create a loving father-son connection. The father thinks, "I work hard every day, and no one appreciates it, not even my son—and I'm doing it all for him."

The son thinks, "Dad doesn't like me, I must be a bad kid, he's an awful father, I hate my life, I feel bad, I don't know what to do now."

Is this really the experience that the man wants to create for his son—or for himself? Of course not. This man works hard every day to protect and nourish his children, and he might even actually lay down his life for them someday. In that stressed-out moment of rushing through breakfast to get to work, however, he doesn't stop and think, "What kind of experience do I want to create for my son, myself, and my family?" He doesn't stop and think at all—he simply reacts. We've all been there.

In previous chapters, we've looked at some of the components of this type of reaction. From chapter 2, for example, we realize that the man could be having a hard day because two or more aspects of his emotional fingerprint are being disrespected.

Maybe he's dreading a day of his boss speaking harshly to him, and his aspects of being trusted, respected, validated, and recognized are being disrespected. Maybe he's worried about not getting enough commissions today, and his aspects of providing for his family and feeling secure are being disrespected. After he snaps at his son, he may feel guilty or confused about why family life seems so hard, and his aspect of being a good parent and being connected to family are disrespected.

In chapters 4 through 6, we saw how important it is to internalize your emotional fingerprint, and we learned what happens when people respond externally instead. When the father snaps at his little boy, he's certainly responding externally. Rather than looking to himself to validate his emotional fingerprint, he's expecting his son to help validate it. When his son spills the milk and makes the father potentially late for work, the father takes it personally. Whatever aspects of his emotional fingerprint needed validation, they didn't get it from his son spilling the milk—and the father isn't validating himself, either. So a little accident seems like a much bigger disaster, especially if the father is stressed, hungry, or not getting enough sleep.

In chapter 7, we saw how FEAR—false evidence appearing real—creates worry, anxiety, and stress, which ups the ante in any situation and makes it more difficult to approach life's wear and tear with perspective, humor, and grace.

In chapter 8, we saw that having expectations is a recipe for frustration. If the father expects his son to be able to avoid spills and accidents, then he's going to be frustrated a lot of the time, since most kids *do* have accidents. If the father expects his son to be extra careful during breakfast time because "Daddy is busy and trying to get to work," then he will often be disappointed, since at least some of the time his son will probably not focus on his father's needs. If the father expects his son to take criticism well and not react badly to being snapped at, he's almost certainly going to be disappointed, since most people—and certainly most children—don't like being snapped at.

Here is this father, trying his best to get himself to work so he can make a better life for himself and his family, and without even thinking about it he's created a bad experience for himself and his family. That wasn't his intention. He would create a better experience if he knew how. As long as he is acting unconsciously and externally, he's going to *react* instead of *decide*.

I sometimes have to struggle not to be that father. Unlike the father in the story, however, I *am* conscious of my emotional fingerprint and I *know* I'm supposed to validate it for myself without expecting my kids to validate it for me. I *know* I'm supposed to replace expectations with standards ("In our house, when you spill milk, you go find a paper towel and mop it up"). Most of the time I'm pretty good at maximizing my emotional fingerprint and creating good—maybe even great—experiences for me and my family.

What happens when I don't? What happens when I slip and catch myself snapping at my kids, arguing with them about cleaning up, or being preoccupied with a work problem in a way that they could easily interpret as my being angry at them?

That's the point at which I realize I need to sharpen my resolve. I need to focus on what's really important to me, decide what kind of experience I want to create, and find a way to begin creating it.

EXERCISE

Finding Your Trigger Points

We often manage to be aware of our emotional fingerprints and to validate them internally—except when we're stressed. Most of us have key trigger points, when we suddenly find ourselves with vastly diminished emotional reserves. Identifying those points for yourself means that you know when to take some extra time to sharpen your resolve, so that you are *responding consciously* instead of simply *reacting unconsciously*.

1. Take a look at the following list. Circle any of the trigger points that weaken your ability to control your responses. Put a star beside the ones that are especially common for you.

- Not enough sleep
- Hungry
- Not enough time to relax
- In pain: headache, backache, sore neck, sore hands, other
- Anxious about work
- Anxious about money
- Anxious about a relationship: spouse, friend, colleague, child
- Transition time: getting ready to go somewhere or just coming back from somewhere
- Noisy environment (especially if you have to raise your voice to be heard, or if you're calling out to someone in another room)
- Too hot or too cold environment
- Someone raising his or her voice
- Someone snapping at you
- Someone crying

2. List any additional trigger points that cause you to be less in control of your responses.

_____

_____

3. Following is a list of options for regaining control of your responses in these trigger situations. Circle any that you think might work for you. Put a star beside the ones that might be especially helpful.
   - Take a deep breath.
   - Drink a glass of water.
   - Count to three, five, or ten.
   - Excuse yourself to use the restroom and take a moment alone.
   - Excuse yourself and take two to ten minutes for a brisk walk—outside, up and down the office stairwell, anywhere you can move quickly and walk off some stress.
   - Try to see the other person's point of view.
   - Try to see the other person as vulnerable and scared, underneath whatever else is going on.
   - Do something nice for someone else.
   - Smile.
   - Tell a joke.

- Think of something that makes you laugh.
- Cry.
- Think of a person, a place, or an image that makes you happy.
- Pray.
- Meditate.
- Repeat a saying that comforts you or amuses you.
- Come up with a word or a saying that reminds you to slow down and take charge of your response.

4. List any additional ways to interrupt a stressful situation that you think might be helpful.

_____

_____

Choosing Your Response

The basic premise of this chapter is very simple: if you don't like what you are experiencing, then do something different.

The "something different" might be mental or emotional. You might simply remind yourself of your emotional fingerprint and take steps to validate two or more of your aspects of importance. You might also internalize your emotional fingerprint by creating a new association. For example, instead of "I hate paying my bills," you might say, "I associate paying my bills with being an adult who has the freedom to make my own decisions, who has a job, and who has some money coming in. This is *so* much better than being a kid and letting my parents make all my decisions about how to spend my money!"

The "something different" might be physical, such as when you are trading emotion for emotion. You might run around the block, call a friend, take ten minutes out to meditate, or fix yourself a healthy snack—anything to give your emotions a chance to reset.

The "something different" might be an action you take with yourself or others, a decision about the kind of experience you want to create. When my wife was having the garage sale, for example, I had a lot of choices about the kinds of action I could take. I might have told her—again!—how much I hate garage sales. I might have gotten in my car and left for the day. I might have pitched in and helped. Or I might have done what I actually did do, which was to find a new way to take advantage of the situation, one that didn't require me to change my long-held aversion to garage sales but that allowed me to have a pleasurable day, too.

In order to shift out of react mode and into the dimension of conscious action, you really need to sharpen your resolve. Most of the time—especially if you're tired, hungry, overworked, or stressed—it feels *much* easier to react unconsciously than to respond consciously. It's much easier to blame the other person—whether that person is a boss, a colleague, or a loved one—for just being wrong and to either vent your frustration or to ask that person to change.

What happens if you sharpen your resolve and find a way to focus on your *own* actions and attitudes rather than the other person's? What happens when you look at the big picture and the long run and choose your response with that perspective in mind, rather than reacting unconsciously out of a momentary annoyance?

In my case, what happened was that I got a wonderful afternoon with my sons and a great date that evening with my wife. Every member of our family had a terrific day. I guarantee you that this would not have happened if I had tried to convince my wife not to hold the garage sale or if I had vented my frustration about her decision to hold it. I thought, "Hmm. Three hours of garage sale versus twenty-four hours of family misery." Put like that, the choice seemed pretty clear.

So if you don't like your experience, do something different— mentally, emotionally, physically, or with another person. Let's break that down, step-by-step.

1. Something negative happens. Ask yourself, "What kind of experience do I want to create?"

   Example: My wife decides to hold a garage sale. I ask myself, "What kind of experience do I want to create?" I realize that I have a choice: be annoyed and frustrated about the garage sale or respond in a different way that will be more satisfying.

2. Accept your emotions.

    Example: Frustrated, annoyed. The worst thing you can do in a situation like this is to lie to yourself about how you feel. Don't pretend that something is all right when it isn't; don't confuse creating a new association (which replenishes your emotional reserves) with talking yourself out of how you really feel (which drains your emotional reserves). In order for me to sharpen my resolve and arrive at a great outcome, I had to be fully in touch with my feelings, not suppressing them.

3. Identify which aspects of importance of your emotional fingerprint have been disrespected.

    Example: Being creative and feeling free and independent. Once you have identified a negative feeling in the previous step, asking yourself which aspects have been disrespected allows you to pinpoint the reason for the feeling. This is empowering, because it leads you to your first choice for taking action.

4. Ask yourself, "Is there a way I could validate myself and end this problem?"

    Example: I asked myself, "Is there some way to be creative today or to be free and independent, regardless of this activity?" I answered, "Not really, because if I shut myself away to paint or if I take off somewhere in the car, my wife will be hurt that I'm completely running out on her project, and I don't want to hurt her feelings. That is not the experience I would like to create." Sometimes you can quickly and easily validate the aspects of your emotional fingerprint that have been disrespected. Sometimes you can't, and you have to take things a step further.

5. Try to create a reassociation (as we learned in chapter 6).

    Example: Maybe I could reassociate garage sales as "My wife is out in the garage doing her thing, and I am hanging out with my boys in the kitchen, cleaning up and getting to spend some quality time with them." That helped some but not enough. Sometimes a reassociation works easily and well.

Sometimes it's not sufficient by itself, so you need the next step.

6. Trade emotion for emotion (as we learned in chapter 7).

   Example: I started doing the dishes and making a game with my boys about how fast we could clean up the kitchen. Again, that helped some but not enough. Trading emotion for emotion is usually very effective, but sometimes it's just not sufficient.

7. Ask yourself if you can replace a frustrating expectation with a newly clarified standard (as we learned in chapter 8).

   Example: In my case, I really didn't expect my wife to give up garage sales. After fifteen years of marriage, I knew better. Maybe I did expect her to "listen to reason," however, or to agree with me if I could just find the right argument to reach her. When I considered switching from expectations to standards, I thought, "This is something she does that annoys me, but how many annoying things have I done over the years that she has never said a word about?" This helped, too, but not quite enough.

8. Before, during, or after the previous seven steps, ask yourself, "What experience do I want to have?"

   Example: When I asked myself this question, my answer was "I want a nice day with my family." This is the part of the process that is really about sharpening your resolve: homing in on what matters most to you. The following chart shows some of the elements that you might take into account.

Elements	Examples
Short-term versus long-term goals	Three hours of a garage sale versus three days of fighting
Close-up versus big picture	Annoyed now versus what she means to me in my life
Path of least resistance versus conscious response	Just reacting versus thinking about what I really want
Blaming another versus taking responsibility	She's ruining my Saturday versus what are my options

9. Before, during, or after the previous eight steps, ask yourself, "What actions do I take to create that experience?"

   Example: The previous step brought everything together for me. I wanted a nice day with my family, and the actions I decided to take were to hang out with my kids and arrange a date with my wife.

When you reach the point of thinking about what actions you want to take, I encourage you to allow yourself to imagine a whole range of possible actions, including some that may seem absurd or outlandish. I was coaching a client who was really frustrated by what he readily agreed was the trivial but still annoying habit of a coworker to keep taking his stapler and then claim that it was hers. He tried all of the ways he could to solve the problem by himself, without bringing it to his coworker, but finally he knew that he would have to do something—he was just too frustrated. To open up the problem and help him to see that he had choices, I encouraged him to really be creative. Here's the list he came up with:

- Steal her stapler and write her a ransom note.
- Buy five staplers in assorted sizes and colors and arrange them all around her desk.
- Yell at her and throw something messy but civilized at her, like confetti.
- Write a singing telegram called "The Ballad of the Stapler Thief" and hire someone to sing it to her.

In the end, he found a package of sticky notes with a picture of a dog on it—he knew she loved dogs—and wrote a note saying, "Please return me to my master, 'cause I can't find my own way home." He put the note in the stapler's "mouth" and left it for his coworker. To his relief, she burst out laughing. Then he handed her a beautifully gift-wrapped box with a stapler inside and said, "So you'll always have your own." She did—most of the time—remember to hold on to hers or to return his.

Always remember that you have choices. It's okay to be creative when you run into a problem with someone else; it might even dissolve the problem. If you don't like the experience you're having, find a way to change it. Turn it into a joke, an adventure, or a missed opportunity.

My wife and I have been talking about one of our sons, who often forgets to do what we tell him. We asked ourselves, "What kind of experience do we want him to have?" and we both realized that we hated the idea that he would see our family as a bunch of people who were always riding him. To create a different experience for our son, we decided, "We're not allowed to give him one criticism until we've given him five sincere compliments." He's happier, we're happier, and it all came from sharpening our resolve to create the experiences that we want.

EXERCISE

Taking Steps

Identify a situation that you currently find frustrating. It could be in your personal life, your relationships, or your work life. Run through the nine-step process with your situation and decide what you want to do about it.

You don't have to wait for something to go wrong to sharpen your resolve. You can also engage in the following steps simply to maximize your emotional fingerprint, however you might choose to do so.

1. Identify something you want.

   Example: To be healthier

2. Identify which aspects of importance of your emotional fingerprint this new desire would meet.

   Example: Feeling confident in my appearance, achieving my life's purpose

3. What will you do *today* to validate each aspect you named?

   Examples:

   Feeling confident in my appearance. Find a gym in my neighborhood.

   Achieving my life's purpose. Find a yoga class in my neighborhood.

4. What will you do *tomorrow* to validate each aspect you named?

   Examples:

   > Feeling confident in my appearance. Visit the gym, check it out.

   > Achieving my life's purpose. Find out what the class costs.

5. What will you do *the next day* to validate each aspect you named?

   Examples:

   > Feeling confident in my appearance. Join the gym.

   > Achieving my life's purpose. Sign up for a class at the gym.

As you can see, you keep adding a new activity for each aspect each day until you have gotten what you wanted or have rewritten your wish. Don't worry about the steps being small. The important thing is to do something each day—and with this plan, you will.

EXERCISE

Moving Forward

Identify an experience you would like to create in your life. It could be in your personal life, your relationships, or your work life. Run through the five-step process with the situation and decide what you want to do about it. You don't have to have a whole plan for getting from where you are now to where you want to be. Just figure out what you're doing one day at a time.

Celebrate Your Emotional Fingerprint

Now you have the necessary tool to internally validate your emotional fingerprint. All that's left is *practice*. If every day you remember your emotional fingerprint, validate and internalize every aspect of importance, and seek to maximize your emotional fingerprint, you'll find yourself reaping extraordinary rewards. When you are faced with challenges and difficulties, you'll be able to tap into a deep well of emotional reserves. When you are living what seems to be an ordinary life, you'll have the resources to make it extraordinary. The power to own your life will be in your hands.

Own Your Life

What would life be without emotion? If you have fear without emotion, it's just a word. If you have love without emotion, it's just a concept. Our emotions are a central part of what makes us human. They fill our lives with sorrow, but they also transform our lives with joy. If emotion is part of the price we pay for our humanity, it is also its greatest reward.

Much of this book has been devoted to the mastery of emotion. Understanding your emotional fingerprint means that you can create your emotional ups and protect yourself from your emotional downs. Letting go of FEAR means seeing clearly past the false evidence appearing real and stepping away from the emotions that the false evidence inspires. Sharpening your resolve means that rather than being overwhelmed by the heat of the moment, you can take a moment to respond and choose what experience you want to create.

All of this work on mastering emotion ultimately has one goal: that you should be able to enjoy and savor every emotion that you choose to own. Owning your life ultimately means owning your emotions as well.

Discovering the concept of the emotional fingerprint and then sharing that with thousands of clients, listeners, and viewers has been an extraordinary journey. I've known fear, grief, anger, and confusion, along with joy, enthusiasm, fascination, and an incredible depth of love. Every step, every emotion, has brought me to the point of sharing what I've learned with you. Because that is what has brought me to this point, I wouldn't give up a minute of it.

Now it's your turn. Go forward into a new, fuller ownership of your life, understanding, internalizing, and maximizing your emotional fingerprint. I wish you every success along the way, and I leave you with the mantra I share with every client:

> I am who I am.
> I will be who I will be.
> Today I am free!

NOTES

Introduction

2 *"The deepest urge in human nature"* Dale Carnegie, *How to Win Friends and Influence People* (New York: Pocket Books, 1982), 19.

5 *"Everything can be taken from a man or a woman"* "Viktor Frankl, from Man's Search for Meaning: Part 1," http://www.pbs.org/wgbh/questionofgod/voices/frankl.html.

2. Master Your Emotional Highs and Lows

55 *"Experimental and clinical psychologists have proven"* Maxwell Maltz, *Psycho-Cybernetics: A New Technique for Using Your Subconscious Power*, http://self-improvement-ebooks.com/books/pc.php.

55 *Some of the most significant research* L. Verdelle Clark, thesis (Wayne State University, 1958), http://hubpages.com/hub/How-to-Improve-Skill-Through-Mental-Rehearsal.

56 *Self-help author James Allen* James Allen, *As a Man Thinketh* (New York: Jeremy P. Tarcher/Penguin, 2009).

61 *"I've learned that people will forget what you said"* Maya Angelou, http://thinkexist.com/quotation/i-ve_learned_that_people_will_forget_what_you/341107.html.

64 *"No matter how busy you are"* "Mary Kay Ash Quotes," http://quotations.about.com/od/stillmorefamouspeople/a/MaryKayAsh1.htm.

3. Embrace Your Emotional Compass

82   *"We can praise God that this ice wall exists"*   Bruce Felton and Mark Fowler, *The Best, Worst, and Most Unusual: Noteworthy Achievements, Events, Feats, and Blunders of Every Conceivable Kind* (Edison, NJ: Galahad Books, 1994), 267.

84   *"As much as the U.S. Navy has shrunk since the end of the Cold War"*   Robert M. Gates, "A Balanced Strategy: Reprogramming the Pentagon for a New Age," January 2009, http://www.dami .army.pentagon.mil/site/dig/documents/Foreign-Affairs-SECDEF-Balance-Dec08.pdf.

4. Discover Your Emotional Reserves

97   *"We who lived in concentration camps can remember"*   "Viktor Frankl, from Man's Search for Meaning: Part 1," http://www.pbs.org/wgbh/ questionofgod/voices/frankl.html.

98   *"As the inner life of the prisoner"*   Viktor Frankl, *Man's Search for Meaning* (New York: Washington Square Press, 1959), 59.

99   *"Out of the night that covers me"*   "Invictus," http://www.bartleby .com/103/7.html.

6. Validate Your Emotional Fingerprint

145   *"If you're going to go through hell"*   "Drew Barrymore Quotes," http://thinkexist.com/quotation/if_you-re_going_to_go_through_ hell-i_suggest_you/203698.html.

7. Clear Your Path

181   *"I've experienced many terrible things in my life"*   "Quotable Quote," Goodreads.com, http://www.goodreads.com/quotes/show/31860.

181   *"Cowards die many times"* William Shakespeare, *Julius Caesar*, act 2, scene 2.

182   *"Anxiety is a thin stream of fear"*   "Roche, Arthur Somers," http:// quotationsbook.com/quote/2645/#axzz1KZWu1iJ7.

183   *"Experimental and clinical psychologists have proven"*   "Latin Dancing in Bed!" http://www.salsabrisbane.com.au/2009/03/latin-dancing-in-bed.html.

198   *"I've missed more than 9,000 shots"*   Hugh Moore, "Michael Jordan Quote on Success," http://www.humorsoffice.com/quotes/ michael-jordan-quote-on-success.

200   *"We must not worry"*   Michelle Klein, *Not to Worry: Jewish Wisdom and Folklore* (Philadelphia: Jewish Publication Society, 2003), xiii.

206   *"Don't ask yourself what the world needs"*   "Empowered Quotes," http://empoweredquotes.com/2009/01/20/harold-whitman-quote.

INDEX